Sex
in the Christian
Marriage

Sex in the Christian Marriage

Richard Meier
Lorraine Meier
Frank Minirth
Paul Meier

SPIRE

© 1988 by Baker Book House

Published by Fleming H. Revell
a division of Baker Book House Company
P.O. Box 6287, Grand Rapids, MI 49516-6287

Spire edition published 1997

Printed in the United States of America

ISBN 0-8007-8644-0

Scripture quotations are from the New American Standard Bible, © the Lockman Foundation 1960, 1962, 1963, 1968, 1971, 1972, 1973, 1975, 1977.

The persons in the case studies discussed represent a composite from the authors' practices. No one individual or couple is portrayed in this volume.

Contents

Introduction

Frank Minirth

What can I add to this book—something medical perhaps? Is the book a little too explicit? Perhaps I can share a case study of some who failed to keep the romance in their marriage and why. Perhaps I can take a more positive approach: a couple that succeeded and why. Whom do I really know that would be a good example?

On and on the thoughts rambled in my head, as I pondered how to write this Introduction. I continued to wrestle with the thought: *What couple do I know that seems really in love?* With some reluctance I thought, Well, *perhaps Mary Alice and I.* No, we are not perfect, but we do seem to have a deep love that is special, and I do continue to view her as though she were my childhood sweetheart.

7

Why am I still romantically in love with Mary Alice and she with me? These are the realizations that come to my mind.

Begin with a Storybook Plot

Many couples can look back and liken the start of their romance to that of a storybook beginning. To one or both of them, their romance was as unlikely as that of Cinderella and her prince or the frog and his princess. Such a beginning was mine. The frog mentality had penetrated deeply into my being.

I had grown up a rather homely sort. In high school I seldom dated. I was very small for my age. In fact, my girl friend in high school was about a foot taller than I and outweighed me by nearly fifty pounds. Not that she was so large—I was just so small. God knew I had some misgivings about this, but it seemed to be the way things were, so I felt I must accept it. I did fight back some, but at four-feet-nine inches and ninety pounds, I had a long way to go, even with my weight lifting. I was definitely not listed in the top three fellows who were in demand to date. In fact, I often identified with an old song that went:

> God gave to the wise men their wisdom,
> To the poets he gave them their dreams,
> To father and mother their love for each other,
> But he left me out, though, it seemed.

After high school, I found college was also rough. My health was poor (mostly because of a serious medical disease—diabetes mellitus) and my height was still short. However, at last I began to grow some and working out consistently began to pay off a little. God was gracious and I began to date more (girls who were closer to my own size now).

God also was gracious in bringing a young minister to room with me at school. He encouraged me daily in Christ, but what got my attention even more was his talk of a brunette journalism major who sat just behind him in class. (I had always been attracted to brunettes.)

One day, at the Baptist Student Union, there she was! My roommate had not introduced me. In fact no one had told me the name of Snow White (that's how she appeared to me). I just knew that this must be the girl he had been talking about. Would she go out with me? Would she even consider it? I probably didn't have a chance—and so the thoughts went.

The B.S.U. was having a Christmas carol sing, and a group of us went. She went also, and my heart thumped with each glance at her dark eyes—but I was with my current girl friend! I did not have any psychiatric training then, but I did know what guilt was. I was with one girl but thinking about another. My best friend had told me about her, so I assumed he also was interested in her. However, I fought off such rational thinking. *Would she dare go out with me?* was the thought that threw off all others.

Well, there was only one way to find out. I picked up the pay phone in the dorm. My hands trembled as I put the coins in the slot. The phone rang. "Hello," she said. My heart jumped when I heard her voice.

I tried hard to fight the quiver in my throat as I attempted to tell her who I was and to ask for a date. She said no. I knew it. I *knew* she wouldn't go out with me. Well, while I had her on the phone, I might as well ask her if she would go out the following week. "Yes." Did she say *yes?* I almost fainted, but I maintained my composure as I coolly told her that I would see her then.

The date worked out fine. Believe it or not, she seemed to like me! At last I could identify with the last verse of that old song:

> I went around broken-hearted,
> Thinking life was an empty affair,
> But when God gave me you
> It was then that I knew
> He had given me more than my share.

I had met a beautiful young maiden and she (though I could scarcely believe it) eventually fell in love with me.

Beauty and the Beholder

Why was I so attracted to Mary Alice? Were there deep subconscious factors generating, of which I was unaware? I believe there were. And this I also believe—beauty is truly in the eye of the beholder.

I believe we tend to be attracted to those who remind us of our parent of the opposite sex. My mother had fine facial features and was of similar stature to Mary Alice. My mother had strong Christian convictions. She never had wealth and always worked hard, but God supplied a sufficient standard of living. In short, to me my mother was pretty, dedicated, gentle, and kind. As I say this, I have to ask myself, Who am I describing, my mother or Mary Alice?

Beauty is only what we perceive it to be. And whom we perceive as beautiful has to do not only with physical characteristics, but also with personality, beliefs, attitudes, background, and deep subconscious factors. A beautiful lady to one man may not be beautiful at all to another.

Background and Its Effect

To those who are not married yet, I would say, consider marrying someone with a background similar to your own. Research shows that marriages that skip more than one social class in a nine-class system usually do not last.

To those who are married and are considering a divorce, I would say, The vast majority of persons I counsel who divorce a mate usually end up remarrying another person of similar personality. The subconscious factors are hard to escape, the negative as well as the positive. For example, why does a woman with an alcoholic father usually marry a man who becomes an alcoholic? Why does she divorce him when he is getting well in therapy, only to marry another man who later also develops an alcohol problem?

To those who are married, I encourage you to remember that beauty is in the mind. It is a highly individual thing and can grow by what we do, which leads to the next point.

How to Run the Race

Just as a storybook beginning can either work for us or be laden with pitfalls, so can the manner in which we live life together: the manner in which we run the race. These factors have helped me.

Mary Alice and I had had two or three dates when I asked her to double with me and go to Memphis, Tennessee, sixty miles away, for supper. We chatted on the way and finally arrived in Memphis. At the restaurant, we were seated and began to eat. I found an appropriate time and took her by the hand. What joy! What bliss! How romantic! But what was this? She took her hand away. (Why? Years later she told me it was sweaty!) However, the flame had been lit. We traveled home, and it began to snow, which was rare for that area. How romantic we both felt. I have never forgotten that evening, and I have never stopped holding her hand.

This book is filled with practical applications. Personal behavior does affect how one feels. Romantic feelings follow romantic behavior.

Husbands: hold her hand, buy her one red rose, give her a big kiss when you walk in the door, look her romantically in the eyes, and tell her she is beautiful. Don't worry about whether or not you *feel* like you are "in love" with your mate today. Instead, behave lovingly toward your mate and the feelings will follow.

Wives: fix up, lose some of that weight, dress seductively for him in private, go ahead and initiate sex (in fact, be aggressive), buy that sexy negligee, wink at him, hold his hand.

How to Finish the Course

However, there are certain pitfalls to avoid, if we are to finish our course together effecively for Christ. These are the pitfalls that seem in abundance today.

Lack of Loyalty

"No, Mary Alice, I was not seeing another girl." We were dating, and she thought I had gone back home to see my old girlfriend. What she didn't know was that I had been in deep theological thought. (In fact, at that point, I was so heavenly minded that I was no earthly good!) I had gone home to have time alone to ponder some deep theological questions. (Boy, if she had only known what she was getting into.) Years have passed. Mary Alice trusts me, and I trust her. At that time, however, we were just dating, but even then loyalty was important. How much more important is it after the two marry, after the two become one?

Perhaps the term *loyalty* is not quite right. Many couples are loyal to a degree, but there seems to be a problem today in having enough loyalty to resist the lust of the flesh.

Joe said he wanted to stay with his wife, June, and the children, but he had fallen romantically in love with Julie. Carol said she was upset with her husband because he was not sensitive to her needs. What she did not tell me was that she was strongly attracted to another man. Only later did this come out. On and on the cases run through my mind. And I grieve as I hear them. There is something very special about being one with only one other person. In a sense, he does become part of her and she part of him. The two are one.

Drive for Material Possessions

The second deadly pitfall is lust of the eyes—*a focus on material possessions.* I must continually remind myself that all the money in the world is not worth the precious time I spend with Mary Alice. I have seen many marriages that started out great, only to fall apart when the drive to feel significant through material possessions led the marriage to destruction. *Relationships* are what have lifelong significance. *Things* do not!

Power Struggles

The third major pitfall is the pride of life—*power struggles.* I am realizing more and more that Mary Alice and I are a team, a team for the Lord. She is, of course, just as important as I. We are both important to Christ. Whatever abilities or assets we have are because of God's grace. I have nothing to boast about. I really have nothing to strive with her about. However, I must still watch my pride of life. Then with Christ and Mary Alice, I will finish the course.

Many readers of this book, in numerous ways, also had a storybook beginning to their marriage. I would encourage them to recall that initial romance with great fondness. Then move on to build a great relationship today. This great drive in humanity—the sex drive—can either make or break a marriage. To ignore it is naive. To misdirect it is destruction. To appropriate it as God's desire in the marriage is to find a hidden treasure. My prayer is that this book will result in some very practical decisions in your search for that treasure.

For further information regarding
the nationwide services of the
Minirth-Meier Clinic, please call

1-800-545-1819

1

Case Studies of
Rekindled Marriages*

God told husbands to

Rejoice in the wife of your youth. As a loving hind
and a graceful doe, let her breasts satisfy you at all
times; be exhilarated always with her love. (Prov.
5:18–19)

I find it hard to believe that God was referring only
to occasional acts of procreation when he said this.
God commanded us, because he loves us, to develop
a healthy, exhilarating sex life with our mate.

*The case studies in this chapter are from the private practice of Dr.
Paul Meier. Names and identifying details have been altered to pre-
serve the privacy of the clients.

And yet, as a Christian psychiatrist, I have seen scores of Christian couples who were going through life missing out on the most pleasurable experience that a loving and imaginative God has created.

Imagine pulling up a comfortable chair as I welcome you to my office. I want to share with you some case studies of couples who have had mild-to-severe sexual conflicts. The purpose is to show you that there is hope for all kinds of sexual problems.

Later chapters communicate how to develop a normal, healthy, sexual relationship with your mate. Chapter 10 gives common questions that couples have in the area of sex. The professional answers are honest and straightforward on this very sensitive subject.

Important Note to Reader

As a Christian psychiatrist, I want to make it very plain that a Christian sex therapist must have extremely high personal ethics. However, I have known some Christian therapists in various parts of the U.S.A. who have lowered their Christian standards and used some nonbiblical techniques practiced by some secular sex therapists. Many sex therapists watch their patients perform sex in their office, for example. This is totally unacceptable. At our clinic, we have over thirty therapists and none of them has been even accused of sexual misconduct—ever. We instruct people verbally. With sexual conflict cases we always try to do conjoint therapy with the husband and wife together.

We are not afraid to give a married woman a

friendly side-by-side hug at an appropriate time, if her husband is also present, or as we are walking out the door with a secretary sitting nearby. But I have seen too many pastors and unskilled therapists who didn't understand the *transference* and countertransference "crushes" that all humans experience from time to time.

It is so easy, as the apostle James said, for us to be enticed by our own lust. "Then when lust has conceived, it gives birth to sin; and when sin is accomplished, it brings forth death. So do not be deceived, my beloved brethren." (James 1:15). Satan also knows where we are weak and would love nothing better than to trip us into some impulsive sin, such as inappropriate sexual conduct with a patient. Then he would trick our depraved minds into rationalizing it and blaming it on some well-known secular sex-therapy techniques. I encourage all pastors and other counselors who are reading this book to be on guard always and watch out for your two worst enemies:

Your own lusts (James 1:15–16), and

The devil, who prowls around like a roaring lion seeking for someone like yourself to devour (1 Peter 5:6–10).

If any reader of this book knows of any secular or Christian therapist who is using sexual misconduct with a counselee, please keep that therapist from damaging fellow human beings psychologically and spiritually. Confront that therapist *with* a witness present. Also, turn that person in to higher authorities in that field, because most of them will either promise to change and not do it, or lie to themselves and justify what they are doing. Sometimes the most dangerous therapists in the world are self-proclaimed, so-called biblical counselors who have not been professionally educated as psychologists or psychiatrists. Christian psychiatrists and psychologists rarely (but I can't say never) slip up sexually. Just remember Jeremiah 17:9, "The heart is more deceitful than all else, and is desperately sick; who can understand it?"

Case Study 1
A Mild Case of Impotence

The Perfectionist

Mr. and Mrs. V. came to my office to share with me that they had been married for fourteen years and until recently had a good relationship, both emotionally and sexually. Mrs. V. stated that even though her husband was somewhat a perfectionist and a mildly workaholic executive, they had still managed to get along quite well. When I asked them what the problem was, Mr. V. said that when he tried to have sex with his wife six weeks before, he was not able to perform. He said that he had remained impotent since that time and was afraid he might never be able to have sex again. He said that this had never happened before.

I asked Mr. V. a series of searching medical and

psychiatric questions but could not come up with any underlying psychiatric problem. In the back of my mind, I was thinking, "Lots of men have one day every year or so when they are physically or mentally exhausted, try to have sex, and just can't get an erection. If they have a healthy self-concept, they will just make a joke about it with their mate, laugh it off, and delay the sexual encounter until the next day.

"But Mr. V. is a perfectionist," I thought. "In fourteen years of marriage, this was his first experience of impotence. Therefore, he has overreacted to this first-time failure, has assumed his sex life is over, and, because of his *fear that he would not be able to perform again*, he wasn't able to. Many men can't sleep at night because they are afraid they won't be able to perform. And some men are impotent merely because they are *afraid* they will be impotent—especially men who are perfectionistic. So I think I'll try *paradoxical intention* on Mr. V."

Paradoxical Intention

This is a psychiatric technique whereby the psychiatrist insists that a perfectionistic person do something that is actually the opposite of what the psychiatrist really wants him to do. The psychiatrist usually tells the person a week or two later what he has done and why he did it. For example, telling an insomniac to stay awake on purpose every night will usually cause him to fall asleep easily. Telling an anxious person to make a list of his worries all day long and then to worry about those items on purpose from 8:00 to 10:00 that night will usually result in the perfectionistic worrier getting angry, throwing away his list, and not worrying for the first time in a long time.

Therefore I told Mr. V. I had a homework assignment for him and that I wanted to see both of them back in my office in one week. His assignment?

1. Do *not* under any circumstance have sex for seven days, and *no* foreplay either.
2. Share gut-level emotions with Mrs. V. twenty minutes every night before going to sleep.

As they were leaving my office, Mr. V. tried to cover up his anger at me, and I could also tell that Mrs. V. was disappointed.

A week later, Mrs. V. came back for their appointment—alone. I asked her where her husband was. She told me that he was too mad at me to come. When I asked her why Mr. V. was mad at me, she said, "Dr. Meier, when you told him last week that he wasn't allowed to have sex for a week, he got so mad that when we got home, we had sex right away. He was able to perform for the first time in six weeks, and we have had sex every night this week."

I then explained *paradoxical intention* to Mrs. V. and how Mr. V.'s anger had overcome his fear. We had a good laugh together.

Case Study 2
Decreasing Performance in Old Age

Mr. N. was seventy-two years old when he came to see my psychiatric associate for the first time.

Mr. N. told him that he and his wife had been married for over fifty years, and that they had had an extremely satisfying sexual relationship. But Mr. N.'s problem was that ever since his seventy-second birthday a month before, his capacity to perform sexually was diminished to about half of what it had been.

My associate promptly told Mr. N. to go home and thank God that at age seventy-two he was able to have sex at all. (In reality, many people are able to enjoy a fun sex life even in their nineties, but one should expect some increasing difficulties as the body gets older, which should not become a matter of concern.)

Case Study 3
The General's Son and Impotence

Mr. and Mrs. C. were a very pleasant Christian couple who were in full-time Christian work together. They were very dedicated to God and to helping others. They had never argued with each other in twelve years of marriage. They were in their thirties and were coming to my office because Mr. C. had been totally impotent for quite some time, and they finally had decided to get therapy as a last resort. Psychological testing revealed that they were both extremely perfectionistic and fearful of intimacy but otherwise they were very emotionally healthy.

Family Background

Mrs. C. was a first-born daughter whose father was perfectionistic but passive in the home, and whose mother was dominant, insecure, and very critical. Whatever Mrs. C. did as a child to please her mother was never quite good enough.

Mr. C. was the first-born son of one of America's top generals. His father was a strict military man who designed a significant portion of America's defense system and expected his home to run like a boot camp. However, whenever the general came home from work, his wife took over as general of the home. She ran the boot camp at home and dominated the general, who had a severe alcohol problem. As a child Mr. C. was never allowed to express any positive or negative emotions. He was taught to "stuff" his feelings and jump to obedience out of pure fear. He was conditionally accepted by his parents, neither of whom ever said, "I love you," or gave him any hugs.

Mr. and Mrs. C. married each other when both were twenty-six years old. They had never analyzed why they had fallen in love with each other, but it was obvious to me that she "fell in love" with him because he reminded her of her passive but perfectionistic father. Mr. C. "fell in love" with Mrs. C. because she reminded him of his perfectionistic but dominant mother.

Transference

As a matter of fact, many of the so-called crush feelings most humans call "falling in love" are no more than an emotional reaction called *transference*. This occurs when he or she meets someone of the opposite sex who reminds him or her of the opposite-sex parent (or, in some cases, of their same-sex parent). This occurs no matter how good or bad that parent may have been.

It was obvious that Mr. C.'s severe impotence was merely a symptom—not the problem. The true problem was all of Mr. C.'s *and* Mrs. C.'s repressed emotions. Having never had any quarrels, both had accumulated lots of unconscious grudges toward each other.

Madonna Complex

Mr. C. had also developed somewhat of a "madonna complex." This means that he felt guilty whenever he tried to have sex with his wife, yet he had no idea why. The unconscious reason for his guilt was that he and Mrs. C. had, over the years, developed such a similar family system to the one they grew up in that he, unconsciously, felt like he was having sex with his mother whenever he was making love with his wife.

Communications Therapy

After giving Mr. and Mrs. C. simple instructions for pleasuring each other sexually, I explained to them that their problem was complex and that Mr. C.'s impotence might not disappear until after nine months to a year of therapy. We worked for forty-five minutes once a week for months purely on their communications skills. They learned to say, "I love you," when they felt any warm feelings toward each other. They learned to hug each other also at these times, even though neither had hugged much as children and both tended to automatically withdraw from hugs.

They learned to say, "I feel angry toward you," whenever one of them offended the other. Whenever one of them felt like giving up and saying, "I just can't communicate my feelings," or, "I can't" *anything*, I had them repeat the same sentence substituting all their "I can'ts" for "I won'ts." I pointed out that whenever Mrs. C. told Mr. C., "You *should*" or "You *shouldn't*" do such and such, she was acting as his mother. She was instructed to replace all her *should* and *shouldn't* messages with "I feel angry toward you when you do or don't do such and such."

After seven months of weekly communications therapy, their marriage improved significantly. Both Mr. and Mrs. C. learned to become aware of a variety of emotions they had incorrectly been forced to repress as children. Both became aware of intense anger toward their parents and learned, with God's supernatural help, to forgive their parents for the parenting mistakes they had made.

Mr. C. became a healthy but not domineering leader in the home. Mrs. C. learned to submit to Mr. C.'s loving and gentle authority and she quit being his substitute mother. Both became healthily assertive in asking for individual needs to be met, but both also learned to get over much of their perfectionism and to *expect a lot less* out of themselves and each other.

"Graduation"

During these first seven months of therapy, the subject of sex was never discussed with Mr. and

Mrs. C. after their first session. I knew that Mr. C.'s impotence was merely a symptom of their faulty communications and family systems' problems, also that his sexual function would automatically revert to normal when his deeper personality problems were resolved. Sure enough, after the eighth straight month of communications and insight-oriented therapy, Mr. and Mrs. C. were all smiles when they came in one week for their usual weekly session. They declared that Mr. C.'s impotence was gone, and that they had enjoyed intercourse several nights that week. After a few more weeks, they were told that they had "graduated" from therapy.

They came back for consultation once every three to six months for a few years, and they have had an excellent marriage since. They have two children now whom they hug a lot, discipline for open rebellion, and encourage to share their honest feelings in a respectful manner. Their children, when they grow up and get married, should have a healthy emotional and spiritual background for a good marriage.

Case Study 4
Father Conflicts

Mrs. H. had never experienced orgasms with her husband. Finally, she got the courage to come and talk to a Christian psychiatrist about it. She enjoyed sex but decided not to go through life missing out on the pleasure of sexual orgasms.

Cause and Effect

It was obvious from the first session with Mrs. H. that the conflicts that blocked her brain from enjoy-

ing orgasms had nothing to do with her husband.
She was fortunate to have a very warm and loving
husband who, unfortunately, had erroneously blamed
himself for not being "man enough" to give his wife
orgasms.

Her conflicts were with her father. Repressed
grudges toward a father are, in my opinion, the primary cause of most instances of failure to achieve
orgasm, the condition known as *anorgasmia*.

Forgiveness

I saw Mrs. H. alone once a week for eight or nine
sessions and probed her mind to get her in touch
with her repressed bitterness toward her father, who
had been a workaholic and had ignored her most of
her life. Only by *forgiving* her father, even though he
might not deserve her forgiveness, could she overcome the psychological/spiritual block to her parasympathetic nervous system (the millions of nerves
God created in each of us that allow us to enjoy the
sexual high peaks called orgasms). After much crying,
ventilating, praying, and *forgiving*, Mrs. H.'s conflicts
toward her father were resolved and she enjoyed orgasms with her husband from then on.

Case Study 5
Overly Victorian Ethics

No Orgasms

Mr. and Mrs. F. came to see me because, even
though they had a great marriage, Mrs. F. had never

experienced orgasms. They had heard, in one of my lectures, that one-third of married women have orgasms during intercourse; one-third of married women have orgasms with finger manipulation by the husband; and one-third of married women never experience orgasms at all. But I also explained in my lecture that *all* married women could probably have orgasms in marriage if they got personal psychotherapy. Some need only a few sessions. Some may need two full years of weekly, insight-oriented therapy.

On psychological testing, Mr. and Mrs. F. both came out, emotionally, very mature and healthy. Both came from excellent, feelings-oriented childhoods. However, Mrs. F.'s childhood was in a home that was very Victorian when it came to sexual issues.

The Taboo Subject

Sex was a taboo subject in her home. Even the word *pregnant* was used rarely and with discretion in the home. Mrs. F., therefore, felt just enough false guilt in her sexual relationship with her husband to block her brain from experiencing orgasms. She enjoyed sex, but never had an orgasm.

After a few weeks of therapy to overcome her Victorian philosophy of sex, Mrs. F. came to see sex from a biblical perspective—that it was a pleasure God intended for all of us to enjoy with our mates. She even studied The Song of Solomon in Scripture. Soon, she was able to experience orgasms with several minutes of finger manipulation by her husband.

Case Study 6
Falling "Out of Love"

Fantasized Sex

Mrs. B. was twenty-three years old, attractive, emotional, and a church organist. She had been married for only two years. She came to my office to inform me that she had decided to divorce her husband, but that her pastor made her promise to come see me for therapy before she saw a lawyer for her divorce. Mrs. B. wanted a divorce because she had "fallen out of love" with her husband. She used to enjoy orgasms with him, but after a year of marriage, she found she could no longer enjoy them unless she secretly fantasized having sex with other men, while actually having sex with her husband.

She especially had sexual fantasies about her pastor, who was a warm and loving man with a degree of charisma. Her vain and naive logic was that since she had "fallen out of love" with her husband, she must not have married the man God intended her to marry. And, since she was "falling in love" with her pastor, he must be the one God originally had intended her to marry (even though he was already married, had three children, and the Bible says that God hates divorce). This is not unusual logic for people who have hysterical (outgoing, dramatic, emotional, self-centered, immature) personality traits, both male and female.

Wise Pastor

Fortunately, her pastor was a mature man who did not yield to her seductions when she went to him for so-called counseling. Politely rebuked by him, she was insulted and surprised that he would not jump at the chance to leave his wife and children and service to God to marry her. Because she had been her father's favorite child all her life, she assumed all other men belonged primarily to her also. Wisely, her pastor persuaded her to seek professional help.

Results of Therapy

It took more than a year of weekly sessions with Mrs. B. to "get through" to her and convince her that she was not quite as spiritual as she had vainly thought. In fact, she became bitterly aware of her own depravity, selfishness, self-righteousness, jealousy, false pride, and rage toward all men for not treating her as her father had done (he had spoiled her severely from her birth and caused most of her problems by doing so). She finally developed some healthy guilt, wept over her sinfulness and false pride, and committed her life to Christ. She also learned to communicate her deepest, inner feelings to her husband, and he became her very best friend. This, eventually, led to feelings of genuine love for the first time in her life.

Transference Crush

You see, Mrs. B. married her husband because he spoiled her, which resulted in her transference crush (some people call this "falling in love") from her father to Mr. B. These romantic feelings lasted through a four-month engagement and one year of marriage (which is about average). But after a year or so of marriage, her depraved, *unconscious* mind realized that her husband was different from her father, so she promptly fell "out of love" and transferred her romantic crush feelings to her pastor, who was very kind to everybody.

Case Study 7
Homosexuality

Temptations

The Rev. J. was a married pastor. He had two children and an exceptionally wonderful wife. But he was secretly homosexual. As a committed evangelical Christian, he had done a pretty good job of resisting his homosexual temptations and had had only two brief homosexual encounters in twelve years of marriage. He had yielded to his homosexual desires only three times prior to marriage. He had never had romantic feelings toward any woman. He married his wife because it was the socially acceptable thing to do, and she was a very nice and talented person.

Mr. J. was a very good person, too. He was a good father to his children. He was very kind to his church members. He loved God. He was so overwhelmed with guilt over his homosexuality that he felt suicidal. He decided it was time to get help.

Homosexuality Foundation

Since I am of the opinion that homosexuality as an *orientation* is laid down in the first six to eight years of life, I began therapy by asking Mr. J. about his early childhood. (Don't misunderstand me.

Homosexual *acts* are definitely a sin and a *choice*. God declares homosexual acts to be against his wishes in both the Old and New Testaments. But having homosexual *inclinations* and temptations is not a sin. These are purely the result of parental child-rearing practices. Homosexuality has *nothing* to do with inherited genes, or variations in hormones.)

Background of Mr. J.

He grew up in the kind of home typical of those from which many homosexuals come (and we have treated hundreds successfully in our clinic). His parents were divorced when he was eighteen months old (before he could identify sexually with his father), so he lived with his mother, his aunt, and his older sister. His father rarely saw him after the divorce. Eighty-five percent of our adult personality traits and orientation are laid down by our sixth birthday, but God can change anything in anyone at any age. Mr. J. identified with his mother from birth on, so inside he felt like a woman. He had feminine characteristics and a feminine orientation. Because of teasing he received from other children in his neighborhood, however, he learned to act more masculine and thus cover up his feminine sexual identity. He craved his father's affection which was a vacuum in his life, and he was jealous of other boys with fathers.

When he reached adolescence, Mr. J. confused his cravings for his father with his new sexual desires. He therefore transferred his crush on his father to other boys with personality traits similar to his father's. Three times he yielded to these homosexual temptations.

False and True Guilt

Overwhelmed with what I consider to be *true* guilt for the three homosexual acts and *false* guilt over his sexual orientation, he decided to live a heterosexual life, even though he was homosexually oriented. He was married to Mrs. J. and felt true guilt over not warning her about his secret homosexual temptations. He had no sexual desires for her, but found that if he fantasized making love to a man while having sex with his new wife, he would have normal male orgasms. However, he had true guilt over fantasizing sex with males.

Over the years Mr. J.'s constant homosexual fantasies made him susceptible to homosexual acts, and twice, on speaking trips, he made homosexual contacts with total strangers. The guilt he felt as a teenager was renewed, and he became suicidal.

Telling His Wife

It took about a year of weekly therapy to cure Mr. J., which is about average for this kind of problem. Since he had a very dedicated wife who would not divorce him under any circumstances, Mr. J. decided to reveal all his secrets to his wife. Sometimes I recommend against this, but this time I agreed. She was upset, grieved, hurt, and angry, but she worked through these feelings and was very supportive of him from then on. Sometimes they came to therapy together, and sometimes he came alone.

He came to realize that his homosexual temptations were only a symptom of his cravings for his father's affection. Since his father refused to have a friendship with him, Mr. J. developed close friendships with two heterosexual males and learned to share gut-level feelings with them. As these friendships grew, his father vacuum shrank, and his homosexual temptations decreased.

Starting Anew

He did not allow himself to have homosexual fantasies. When he sometimes slipped on this (just as we all do occasionally with our heterosexual temptations), he asked God to forgive him for having dwelt on his fantasies, and then he forgave himself. For a while, he was unable to have orgasms with his wife, but gave her orgasms through finger manipulation. Eventually, as he shared more and more gut-level feelings with her and became more emotionally intimate with her, he began having orgasms with her again (this time, without homosexual fantasies). He even developed some genuine romantic feelings toward her.

I have seen Mr. and Mrs. J. once every six months or so for many years now, and they are both serving God faithfully and have a happy marriage. During times of crisis or times of personal insecurity (like we all have), Mr. J. occasionally will still have homosexual temptations, but now he knows *why* he has them, and he knows he isn't sinning as long as he doesn't dwell on them. He will never again yield to those temptations with any actual homosexual acts; I feel certain of that.

Case Study 8
The Dangers of Romanticism

Midlife Crisis

Mrs. W. was a forty-five-year-old romantic in mid-life crisis. She had been a fairly committed Christian since her teenage years, but she spent a great deal of time almost every day watching daytime and nighttime soap operas, reading dramatic romantic novels, and going to romantic movies.

She served God by singing in the choir, teaching Sunday school, and being kind to her neighbors. She even led a number of neighbors to a personal relationship with the Lord Jesus Christ. But Mrs. W. spent a great deal of time in personal fantasy. Since childhood, she based too much of her self-worth on her good looks. She fantasized being a queen. She fantasized having a husband who existed primarily for her, who brought her poems and flowers weekly, and who always wanted to listen to everything she was thinking or feeling.

There aren't any men like that (except while they are courting a woman)! Or if there are, they are rare. They exist only in novels, soap operas, and movies. But poor Mrs. W. didn't know that, so she accumulated more and more grudges toward Mr. W., who was really an exceptionally good husband, but he didn't think about giving his wife flowers or surprising her with other small gifts.

The Flame Rekindled

Mrs. W. decided to divorce him and find another husband—you know, the kind that exist in the novels and soap operas. Fortunately, her friends talked her into getting therapy, where she gained insights into her own vanity and depravity, repented, and began to realize what a great husband she really had. Her sex life improved again. By *behaving lovingly* toward her husband, even though she had fallen "out of love" with him, her *feelings of love* returned little by little. But this time, they were for real.

Case Study 9
The Consequences of Abortion

False Reasoning

Daily thousands of women have an abortion. They are duped by a godless society into thinking that an abortion is no more than "eliminating a blob of meaningless cells" from their bodies—something they say they *should* do if it is an *inconvenience* in any way. Some women liberationists who *say* they believe this know deep in their minds that they are wrong. They devote much energy in vain attempts to prove they are right. All the time they know they are killing a human life and that it is morally wrong, but they use massive denial to cover up their sin and guilt. As a result, they suffer lifelong psychological consequences for that sin, unless they get good Christian therapy and admit the truth, confess it, and forgive themselves.

Relatively "Moral" Non-Christian

One example of such a woman was a hospital patient whom I will call Mrs. T. She was not a Christian, but she was a *relatively* moral non-Christian. While growing up, she went to a liberal church occasionally, was nice to her friends, didn't take drugs, and got decent grades in school. She didn't go to bed with boys she dated, as a rule, but twice she did become sexually involved with boys during her college years. Both times she came close to being engaged, had sex, got pregnant, and had an abortion (with the advice and consent of the college psychologist).

She rationalized these abortions and repressed her guilt, but it plagued her unconscious mind for many years to come. Later, she married a third young man, had two children, and lived a relatively normal life in society. But her unconscious guilt blocked her ability to have orgasms. She had bouts of anxiety and depression from the guilt, but she had *no* idea why the anxiety or depression was there.

The Trigger Event

Ten years after the marriage, when the oldest daughter was eight years old, a very senile old man in their neighborhood tried to fondle Mrs. T.'s eight-year-old daughter. The eight-year-old ran away from him immediately and told her mother.

Any normal mother would be bothered a great deal by this. Most would get angry and make sure that a closer eye was kept on a ninety-one-year-old man out walking who no longer had control of his impulses, but because of all her repressed sexual and abortion guilt, Mrs. T. overreacted, went into a rage, and became totally psychotic that same day. She was brought to our psychiatric ward in the hospital. For days she didn't know who she was and had gross delusions (believed things that weren't true) and hallucinations (thought voices that no one else heard were calling out to her).

She was cured of her psychosis with a few days of medication on major tranquilizers (which restored her brain's dopamine levels back to normal so that the delusions and hallucinations would go away). Then I carefully probed her thoughts to find what crises in her past could have set her up for this kind of psychotic reaction. I knew it was probably related to sexual guilt by the mere logic that a sexual event (the fondling of her daughter) triggered it.

Admission and Forgiveness

At first, Mrs. T. denied having any sexual guilt. But later when asked more detailed questions about her past she finally admitted the two abortions. When she did, she burst into tears and wept for hours.

It was then that she asked Christ into her life, asked God to forgive her, and began the process of forgiving herself. She decided to keep her abortions a secret from her husband and friends, which I considered a wise choice. She had admitted it to God and had forgiven herself, and God had forgiven her. After three weeks of daily therapy in the hospital, she was completely recovered. Her daughter also saw a counselor to discuss her feelings about the old man, just to be sure she would carry no psychological scars.

Case Study 10
Sadomasochism Is Curable

Mrs. E. grew up with an alcoholic, abusive father, who abused her both psychologically and sexually while she was growing up. She hated him for this, but nevertheless craved his affection, since he never gave her any true tenderness.

Sadist Transference

As a teenager, Mrs. E. always had transference on men who were physically and sexually abusive and who took drugs, as would be expected. (As crazy as it sounds, that's the way our depraved brains happen to work!) At age eighteen she married one of these fellows, who never got a job, ran around, beat her during sex, and was an alcoholic. She worked to support the family, even after having children.

"For Jesus"

Mrs. E. was a Christian but not a very insightful one. She was a masochist. Because of her childhood, she felt comfortable only when she was "suffering for Jesus."

Mr. E. was a sadist—he enjoyed hurting people, especially women, because of the sick relationship with his mother he had while growing up. Mrs. E. went to prayer meeting every Wednesday night and requested prayer for her poor alcoholic, abusive husband. Everybody at church thought, "What a saint Mrs. E. is to put up with all that suffering for Jesus."

Little did they know that the suffering wasn't really for Jesus. She was merely continuing in her family system because that's what she had become used to. One day Mrs. E.'s pastor decided to talk to Mr. E. Surprisingly, Mr. E. became a Christian, got into therapy with a Christian counselor, matured rapidly, became a good husband and father, and was rapidly promoted in the job he acquired.

Four years after his conversion, Mr. E. was a leader in the church and owned his own very successful business. God blessed him tremendously.

Near-Disastrous Result

What do you think happened to Mrs. E? Most naive humans would assume that she was delighted and lived happily ever after. But any trained psychiatrist knows that in over half of cases like this one, the wife will divorce her cured husband and marry another abusive, alcoholic husband to keep her family system going, while having no understanding why she is doing so. And that's what almost happened.

First, Mrs. E. became suicidally depressed because unconsciously she could no longer justify the bitterness she harbored toward her father and Mr. E. Then she got hooked on prescription drugs and began having affairs with alcoholics she picked up at bars. She came to our psychiatry unit suicidal.

After two months of daily therapy in the hospital, Mrs. E. gained enough insights into her own depravity to give up her masochism. She learned also to accept the fact that God loves her and that she *deserves* to have a good husband (because of God's grace) and a *fun* sex life, *with him*, free of sadomasochism.

I could relate hundreds of cases on sexual conflicts of various sorts, but you have gotten the picture that will enable you to begin your own journey into yourself. Consider counseling sessions with a Christian psychiatrist, psychologist or marriage counselor. It's a scary journey, so don't try it without Christ in your life. Trust his death on the cross and resurrection power to cleanse you of your guilt and to give you eternal life to replace it. Then dedicate your life to serve God and to enjoy that service. Christ came to earth so we could experience an abundant life (*see* John 10:10). A good sex life with your mate brings pleasure also to the God who created you.

2

Rekindling the Flame

The Flame Is Needed

Importance of Romance

Throughout a married couple's life the flame of romantic sex should continue to burn. Without romance, the total sexual experience loses sparkle and becomes boring and tedious, when it was meant to be fun-filled, exciting, exhilarating, and totally fulfilling.

Romance is the *fun* of sexuality and leads to actual intercourse. Romance is something that should be expressed throughout the day—not just in the bedroom—and it should continue throughout the marriage.

Unfortunately, this concept is not accepted by all couples, especially by those having problems in some area. It is indeed sad to hear statements from couples who have been married twenty, twenty-five, thirty, or more years, as they describe their sex life. "You can't expect too much after forty" . . . "Things start falling apart as you get older" . . . "We just can't cut the mustard any more, it seems."

Not the Norm

In counseling we discover that problems in the area of romantic sex are accepted—almost fatalistically—as normal, as if there were no hope for solving them and keeping the flame of romantic love continuing in the more mature years of marriage. This need not be so. Such couples need to look at their attitudes and change their ways of thinking to line up with God's ways.

Various factors contribute to why a husband or wife or both do not have a proper emphasis on the romance of sex. Many Christian couples view sex as a "need-to-do" instead of a satisfying pleasure. This view may have developed as a result of rigid rules in childhood or in college, from an absence of positive input from the church about sex in marriage, or from a lack of instruction at home regarding full sexuality. As a result many Christian couples are living unfulfilled sexual lives and are missing out on the joy that God has for them in the marriage relationship.

What Does the Bible Say

God's Word places great importance on romantic sex in marriage. God invented sex. It was God who commanded Adam and Eve to be fruitful and multiply. They, no doubt, enjoyed romantic sex in the Garden of Eden long before any children came along. God intended sex to be for their fulfillment and enjoyment.

With reference to romantic sex, King Solomon, author of much of Proverbs, said, "Let your fountain be blessed, and rejoice in the wife of your youth. As a loving hind and a graceful doe, Let her breasts satisfy you at all times; Be exhilarated always with her love" (Prov. 5:18, 19). The King James Version of the *Bible* uses the word *ravished* in the place of *exhilarated*. The word in the original means *intoxicated*. In other words, sex is not something that is a burden or duty to be performed at a low moment of life. Rather, it is a privilege and thrill given by God with his direct command and with the expectation that the enjoyment of it should be an intoxicating experience of pleasure.

The writer of Hebrews says, "Let marriage be held in honor by all, and let the marriage bed be undefiled" (Heb. 13:4). The bed and the activities on the bed, which have a direct reference to romantic sex, are pure and sinless.

Dr. and Mrs. Ed Wheat declare:

not only was it [the sexual relationship] meant to be a wonderful, continuing experience for the husband and wife, but it was also intended to show us something even more wonderful about God and His relationship with us. Ephesians 5:31, 32 spells it out: "For this cause a man shall leave his father and mother, and shall cleave to his wife: and the two shall become one flesh. This mystery is great; but I am speaking with reference to Christ and the church." *Thus, the properly and lovingly executed and mutually satisfying sexual union is God's way of demonstrating a great spiritual truth.* It speaks to us of the greatest love story ever told—of how Jesus gave himself for us and is intimately involved with and loves the Church. ... In this framework of understanding between two growing Christians, the sexual relationship can become a time of intimate fellowship as well as delight.[1]

The apostle Paul, in describing the continuity of the practice of sex in the life of a Christian couple, warned about depriving one another of this beautiful privilege. He said, "Stop depriving one another, except by agreement for a time that you may devote yourselves to prayer, and come together again lest Satan tempt you because of your lack of self-control" (1 Cor. 7:5).

Common Obstacles

New situations certainly may develop as a marriage continues over the years, but these are not reasons for the flame to flicker. Instead, these new challenges should be faced with a positive attitude, rather than taken as an unrealistic signal that this phase of marriage is now on the decline or over.

Some examples of common obstacles that can develop through the years of marriage and that can

1. Ed and Gaye Wheat, *Intended for Pleasure* (Old Tappan, N.J.: Fleming H. Revell Co., 1981), p. 22.

interfere with a happy sex life are: physical or mental sickness; fear of failure; problems relating to over-eating or drinking; boredom; preoccupation with economic difficulties; problems on the job; mental or physical fatigue; inability to let oneself completely go during romantic sex; unresolved feelings of resentment, and lack of concern for the spouse's satisfaction during sexual intercourse.

These should be seen as challenges that can be resolved if the couple is interested in facing them squarely and realistically with the goal of keeping the flame of love burning throughout all the years of their marriage.

The Continuing Sex Drive

Getting older doesn't need to be a threat to the flame of love, even though the sex drive does decline with age—a fact that needs to be reckoned with. In a man, this decline begins in the twenties and continues gradually until about age sixty. The rate of decline then decreases. In a woman, there is usually no significant decline until about age sixty and, even after that point, the decline is gradual.

There is no valid reason why a normal couple cannot continue enjoying romantic sex well into their older years, especially if they try to adjust to the various changes that age may bring to their natural sexual response.

The sexual response of most women is less affected by age than is that of their husbands. In older women, however, sexual arousal takes longer and the excitement plateau is more rapidly completed. Menopause does not normally reduce a woman's sex drive. Even if it seems to in some women, it is only a temporary condition.[2]

Some statistics show that 73 percent of men are still sexually potent at age seventy. When this is not the case, there is usually a psychological rather than a physical reason.[3]

The familiar phrase "Use it or lose it" is a good one to apply to the subject of romantic sex. Continued sexual activity is the best guarantee that the couple will continue to enjoy the pleasures of romantic sex through middle age and even beyond.[4]

Dr. and Mrs. Herbert J. Miles point out that "often when the sex life of a couple ceases at sixty or before, the reason is that husband and wife are in basic emotional conflict over childish common trifles. . . . When husband and wife are committed to each other in full Christian love in its broad sense, marriage is first, last, and always a sexual relationship between husband and wife."[5]

Why the Flame Flickers

Where Did Romance Go

A primary cause for the flame of sexual love to flicker is a lack of emphasis on the *romance* of sex.

2. Diagram Group, *Sex: A User's Manual* (New York: G. P. Putnam's Sons, 1981), p. 135.

3. Ibid., p. 122.

4. Robert E. Dunbar, *A Doctor Discusses a Man's Sexual Health* (Chicago: Budlong, 1976), p. 118.

5. Herbert J. and Ruth Harrington Miles, *Husband-Wife Equality* (Old Tappan, N.J.: Fleming H. Revell Co., 1978), p. 151.

As a married couple gets older, such a lack becomes much more apparent and begins to bring negative factors into the relationship.

Our research shows that a wife's most common criticism of her husband's standard type of lovemaking is that he is too preoccupied with the mechanics of intercourse, to the point that he really ignores what turns his wife on romantically—total body sensuality.[6] His focus, too often, is merely on intercourse and *his* orgasm, to the exclusion of whole-body love play, which is essential to his wife.

To paraphrase one woman, who discussed her sexual taste in *The Hite Report*, lovemaking is at least 75 percent sensuality and, at most, 25 percent sexuality. Unfortunately, many men reverse the proportions and place their emphasis on sexuality.[7]

On the other hand, many husbands, when analyzing their sex life, complain that their wives are not very responsive. Of course, the husband may need to bear part of the blame for this. Because of the lack of romance and preparation he gives his wife, she may find it hard to get into the mood for intercourse so that she will want to respond.

Whole-body Love Play

This activity generally needs to be emphasized in a new and greater way as a couple gets older. It must be stressed that whole-body love play must be done

6. Michael Castleman, *Sexual Solutions* (New York: Simon and Schuster, 1983), p. 162.
7. Ibid.

at a leisurely pace—not in a hurry. The basics of sex
may do for a while for a young couple, but romantic
sex is where the flame burns for mature couples.

A variety of additional flame quenchers also can
creep into the sex life. We will deal with some of
these in greater depth later, but let's review some of
them here.

1. *Emotional factors* may include depression; low
   self-esteem; anger over festering hurts or misunderstandings; fears of failure, of pain, or of
   becoming pregnant; performance anxieties; an-
   noyances, such as children still being up during
   sex, squeaky beds, uncomfortable temperature
   factors, or the phone ringing; bitterness over
   accumulated verbal abuses and insults; intim-
   idations one toward another that would make
   either partner no longer feel valued or loved;
   and false guilt experienced by some who have
   been brought up in Victorian Christian homes
   that did not have balanced information on the
   subject of sex.
2. *Mental preoccupations* may include concerns
   that carry over from the job; Monday-night
   football; or fears of a family member wandering
   into the bedroom.
3. *Physical obstacles* may include fatigue; the action of the digestive processes immediately following a large meal (which uses energy that
   otherwise might be available to enjoy a high
   energy level of sex); overweight; being in poor
   physical shape generally; and some sicknesses
   or diseases.

4. *Sexual behavior deficiencies* may dampen the flame of romantic sex, factors such as inadequate understanding of one's own genitals and those of one's partner; inhibitions; a lack of imagination in sex play; a lack of tenderness and sensitivity in touching and caring; lack of communication before and during sex; and a failure to know one's partner's sexual needs.

Ideas for Turning on the Flame Again

The How-tos

The flame is romance. Therefore, the couple needs to relate to each other's emotional and affectional levels.[8] There needs to be the expression and experience of feelings of warmth and tenderness while caressing each other's body. A couple should enjoy cuddling and kissing without this necessarily leading to intercourse. In fact, some wives enjoy kissing and cuddling as much as actual intercourse.

True romance means and includes mutual gratification. Most husbands want their wives to understand that sex is getting as well as giving. It *is* mutual gratification. Husbands want to give love, but they also want to receive love. Making love shouldn't be seen as something that happens to you, but something that you should make happen to the other person. Making love focuses on the physical expression of closeness between two souls, not just the connection between the sex organs.[9]

8. Leo I. Jacobs, *Overcoming Impotence* (Chicago: Contemporary Books, 1978), p. 14.

9. Castleman, *Sexual Solutions*, pp. 16–17.

Little Things Mean a Lot

Romance is something that should be expressed throughout the day, not just in the bedroom. It is the practice of tenderness, affection, respect, and kindness, along with signals of sensuality. The wife, especially, needs to receive little expressions of romance throughout the day whenever the husband is at home. As the husband learns to express feelings and to share sensuous touchings, he will discover that, as his wife reciprocates, he will enjoy those things that she discovers please him.

> To keep romance in marriage, show small courtesies to one another. Wait on one another, open doors, give up the easy chair, sew on buttons, carry burdens, serve a cool drink of water, be helpful. Kind deeds stoke the cooling fires of romance into mature, tender expressions.
>
> Husband and wife need to communicate in gentle affectionate words. If the meal was good, say so. Call each other by your pet names. . . .[10]

Romance includes the way a husband surprises his wife with creative gifts. He can call her from work; he can become a specialist on what makes his wife want to make love. She needs to want to make love first. This means her desire must be primed for it through the husband's tenderness, caring, kissing, and touching that he expresses outside of bed. She needs to get into the mood for sex.

10. Miles, *Husband-Wife Equality*, p. 156.

Be Prepared

Mental preparation is called *seduction*. Physical preparation is called *arousal*. Seduction can include candlelight, flowers, soft music, gently taking off each other's clothes, and kissing and touching each other as this process continues. Making some of the times of lovemaking extra-special events is a way of staging romance. A couple might stage two very special events each week. The one event could be a "his-needs party," especially relating to the needs of the husband; the second should be a "her-needs party," especially catering to her particular needs in the area of romance and sex.

Special times together are seen as being very romantic, especially to the wife. A wife calls a special dinner romantic. Walking through a park, alongside a lake, through the woods, or through a shopping mall may be romantic to her. Such is a time for communicating, caring, and sharing intimacy, all wrapped up in one.

Someone once said that sex is something you do with an organ; love is something you do with a person. Love is feeling close emotionally, even when you don't feel like having sex. Love is having better sex because you do feel close emotionally.[11] It is *romance* that keeps the flame burning.

Importance of Communication

Communication during romantic sex is important, especially to the wife. Most women desire more com-

11. Michael Morgenstern, *How to Make Love to a Woman* New York: Ballantine Books, 1982), p. 6.

munication than they get. The best subjects a man can talk about then are qualities about her that he likes; things that are personal; intimate; what feels good; encouragements (never demands); expressions of what gives pleasure; and gentle instruction if she asks. Talking is important during lovemaking, while cuddling, during sex, and afterward. Positive communication during lovemaking includes, of course, compliments, which should be accepted (not shunned or disagreed with). There needs to be that feeling of acceptance, warmth, intimacy, and caring. The worst thing a man can do immediately after sex is to roll over and go to sleep without saying anything!

Discussion after sex *should not involve any difficulty that may have developed during sex*. The best time to solve sexual difficulties is outside of the sexual context.[12] Freedom to share such feelings or inhibitions with each other is very important, but the best time is at a separate setting.

Creativity in Romance

The flame of romance is fueled by creativity. Some suggestions in this area are: sleep together in the nude; develop new positions and variations in intercourse; move out of the bedroom for sex; or play games related to seduction. These actions develop an intensely passionate time together and can produce a humorous and relaxing atmosphere. One of the games could include striptease on the part of one or both partners. Creativity with seductive clothing can

12. Ibid., pp. 80–81.

help return the proper erotic thoughts and desires in each other's mind and heart and stimulate passion for each other.

Have an enthusiasm for each other. A wife especially wants her husband to have an eagerness as well as excitement for life and for the relationship. A good sense of humor adds fuel to the flame.

Grooming and Fitness

There should be a dedication to good personal physical conditioning and grooming. Bathing or showering before intercourse shows the partner how important this act of love means to him or her. Shaving at night shows the wife how her husband values this closeness. Good physical conditioning prepares the body for lovemaking, whether it is a brisk walk together, riding an exercise or regular bicycle, or joining a "Y" fitness program. These activities will help not only your physical appearance but also ready you for sex play.

Making time, (instead of finding time) is also important for fueling the flame of romantic love. What are your *real* priorities? It is most important to make time for whatever matters most to you. Most people get so chronically bogged down with appointments and commitments that their romantic love life is squeezed out into the unimportant category.

Make Special Plans

Plan time alone together. Can you remember the last time the two of you were home alone together for a whole evening? Whenever you can, get a friend or relative to take the children out of the house so the two of you can have the evening alone in your own home.

Good lovers avoid boredom in their routine. Go to a motel overnight without the children. This would certainly seem appropriate to celebrate a wedding anniversary.

Your Sexual Self-Esteem

Feeling good about yourself sexually is important in refueling the flame. Accept compliments that are given you by your mate. Do not reject them. Do not pretend to be overly modest and humble. If one partner says, "You look handsome," or "You look beautiful," don't disagree. Instead say *thank you* and start *acting* like you feel good about yourself. If you do not agree with the other person about his or her compliments, at least give your partner the freedom to think differently than you and to have different tastes than you have.[13]

Sometimes there are misconceptions about what is really attractive to the other partner. Many wives feel inferior because they do not have the attractive shape that they think they should have, especially in breast size. However, it is very interesting to discover that in a national survey taken in Great Britain, husbands rated the most physically attractive attribute of their wives to be their face, not their breasts. The eyes, in particular, were chosen by 62 percent of those

13. Theresa Larsen Crenshaw, *Bedside Manners* (New York: Mc-Graw-Hill, 1983), p. 56.

who were asked what was the most important feature of attraction. The hair came in a close second. In a similar survey, the top attributes most appreciated by men were the woman's face (32 percent), legs (24 percent), bust (18 percent), and hair (5 percent).[14]

To feel good about yourself sexually, you must have an underlying faith that romantic sex is God's will for you and your partner. Sex is more than just having children. It is rendering due benevolence. It is meeting the real needs of each other (1 Cor. 7:4). Romantic love play is a good description of sex in Christian marriage. It is that capacity of enjoyment given by God in which the couple can relate in deep communion with one another at this important level. It should be seen as fun and excitement instead of duty and boredom. It should be the highlight of a couple's life together.[15]

14. Diagram Group, *User's Manual*, pp. 50–51.
15. Wheat, *Intended for Pleasure*, p. 236.

3

How Wrong Emotions Can Affect Sex

One of the major emotions in satisfying romantic sex is *eros* love, which is the feeling element of wholesome love. Wrong emotions can very easily damage this fragile feeling of love. When a couple says "We have lost our love for each other" (the second leading excuse for divorce), what they usually mean is that they have lost their *feelings* of love for each other. They may say this reason in other ways, such as, "We have fallen out of love," "We now love each other as brother and sister instead of husband and wife," "We are going through the motions but our hearts are not in it," "It seems like a wall has developed between us," or "It seems like the chemistry is gone. We are not attracted to each other as we used to be."

Occasionally *any* couple senses a loss of emotional intimacy, that is, the loss of feelings of love. This may last a day or even several, depending on a number of stressful factors. If it lasts more than two weeks, marriage counseling is needed to discover the problem, to identify which wrong emotions or behaviors block this emotional intimacy.

Where do we begin to look for these blocks?

Unresolved Anger

Unresolved anger may be in the form of open hostility or buried resentment—including the recurrence of little resentments thought not important enough to discuss with a spouse. Little resentments can build, layer on layer, to produce a wall, blocking the ability to experience *eros* love fully.

Case Study—Anger

A couple who had been married only a year came in for counseling. The husband felt he had lost his feelings of attraction and love toward her, and he was also experiencing impotence. The underlying problem, however, turned out to be unresolved anger in the form of resentment. The husband had carried an unwritten rule in his mind since they first married that they both should control their weight. Through the course of their first year of marriage, however, the wife had put on about ten extra pounds.

The husband indicated that he felt this was a small issue (which, of course, was true) and therefore wasn't worth talking about. Because of the strength of the rule that he had made internally, however, and his wife's apparent violation of it, he had developed resentment toward her. As the resentment built, layer on layer, it developed enough strength to effectively block his feelings of love and attraction toward his wife. When he admitted this problem, his wife shed a few tears and apologized for not taking care of herself as he had assumed she would. He apologized for having such unrealistic expectations. Having talked it out in the counselor's office and again at home, that same evening they experienced good, romantic sex again. The block had been removed.

Anger blocks are often a result of an individual's perfectionistic and unrealistic expectations. Anger is often perpetuated by a drive for vengeance and an unwillingness to assertively discuss one's feelings and then to forgive.

Any time anger or other emotions dominate a person's mental focus, most expressions and experiences of emotional intimacy are shut down. Strong negative emotions and emotional intimacy can rarely coexist. When they collide, it is like a small Volkswagen crashing into an eighteen-wheeler diesel truck. The Volkswagen suffers the most damage.

Our fragile but retrievable capacity to empathize and to feel love is often curtailed when unresolved anger blurs our mental focus. We protect our security under such conditions with distance and separateness ("Don't touch me," "Leave me alone"). When we remove the wreckage of these wrong emotions, then our sense of security once again can be enhanced by togetherness and intimacy.

Unresolved anger sometimes may be associated with the death of a friend or relative. It also may exist because of a job loss, hurts, or other misunderstandings. Anger, no matter how it is veiled, will definitely affect intimacy in sexual love. Sexual boredom is often a cover-up for pent-up, improperly expressed rage or anger over issues that were not resolved verbally when they first occurred.

Using a make-believe politeness or trying to forget those hurts will not remove them from the seething kettle inside us.

If a man has a dominant wife whose control he resents, his anger concerning this characteristic may create a complete *lack of interest* in sex as a way of retaliating. He may not do this necessarily in a conscious or malicious way, but his anger will affect his sex life indirectly.

Sometimes, through anger or revenge, a wife may use *sexual rejection* as a weapon. She thinks she is getting even with her husband by releasing this nuclear bomb, but *she* is the one who loses. A fallout usually poisons her own chances for sexual satisfaction.[1]

A man who loses his temper easily and loudly expresses anger intimidates his wife. She loses her feelings of being treasured, loved, and valued. Her tenderness and softness can turn to *hurt* and *with-*

1. David Reuben, *How to Get More Out of Sex* (New York: David McKay Co., 1974), p. 42.

drawal. She may be nice to him on the outside, because of her fear of his temper, but she will stop communicating sexually and often wwll lose her desire to respond to him altogether.[2]

On the other hand, a husband can become a "peacemaker-at-any-price" type of man. His wife can criticize and nag him, and it may not seem to bother him outwardly. But inwardly he cringes. He doesn't like the way he is being treated. His ego is being hurt. His peacemaking desire may drive him to attempt to overlook the little things that are not worth making into major issues. His bottled-up feelings, however, may show in the *loss of an erection* during sex. His stored frustrations and resentments can make sex unattractive to him.[3] His anger can quench the sex drive that he once had.

Loss of feelings of love and sexual inability because of anger and depression need be only a temporary situation, if the couple is willing to work on the cause of this emotion. The only way to deal with anger properly is to verbalize it. Communicating pains and hurts at a proper time, in an acceptable manner, can lead to resolving issues. A good, healthy self-acceptance should enable a person to develop communication skills with which to express both positive and negative thoughts while at the same time, accepting personal weaknesses. In this way, the discussion can be seen as an act of self-revelation rather than of exposure which might lead to rejection.

2. Crenshaw, *Bedside Manners,* pp. 71–72.
3. Ibid., p. 72.

Anxiety

Another wrong emotion that can block sexual intimacy and the feelings of love is the emotion of anxiety.

A. Wife's Anxieties

Sexual attractiveness. Some anxieties a wife may have include the belief that she is not attractive to her husband, is not sexual enough for him, or that he might reject her. Wives need to realize that what a husband appreciates most is not a wife with perfect features but one who feels at home with herself. In fact, eight out of ten men in a *Redbook* survey said they were more excited by "A woman who loves me" than by one having large breasts or some other special physical feature. A husband knows a wife feels good about herself when she projects her feeling of love for him. The usual problem is that a wife does not know how her husband feels about her, so she feels uncertain about herself. If a husband would let his wife know what he appreciates about her, she would feel better about herself and would be much more at ease in their sexual relationship.

Sexual ability. The wife may have anxieties about her sexual prowess. She may fear she will not have an orgasm, that her orgasm will come too soon or take too long, or that she may become exhausted during intercourse. A woman may have anxiety because her husband may want her to do something she does not want to do or is afraid to try. A wife should not feel pressured into doing anything she does not feel comfortable with or have a clear conscious about. Reading a sexual technique manual and communicating feelings and ideas gained from such reading is a good project for couples in this situation.

Possibility of pregnancy. Many wives have anxieties about becoming pregnant. If so, some definite and safe method of birth control should be used to reduce this fear to a minimum.

After surgery. A woman may have anxieties connected with her health, for instance, recent hysterectomy, which should not be a hazard or a deterrent to a couple's sex life. Most difficulties that arise as a result of such surgery come only from a lack of understanding. There also may be anxiety connected to wrong information, such as the myth that sexual interest and capability decrease dramatically after menopause. The truth is that romantic sex can be just the same or even better for a postmenopausal woman, if she is comfortable with herself and well-adjusted to her husband.

A Husband's Anxieties

Sexual performance. A common anxiety for a husband is that he will lose his erection. He works hard at being a good sexual performer but hard work takes away from the fun of sex. He forgets to use his sense of humor and to be playful. He turns pleasure into duty and enjoyment into goals that put him under pressure. He needs to relax and to enjoy the pleasure of romantic sex rather than to try to perform.

Sensitivity to distractions. The ringing of the phone or a doorbell or the sound of footsteps coming near the bedroom can contribute to a loss of erection and a block to the sense of sexual attraction. Some thought may suddenly burst into a husband's memory—a forgotten birthday, an anniversary or something else totally unrelated to the present moment. These or other external or internal distractions can make the feelings of love and the success of the sexual experience disappear for many men.

Physical Health. Sometimes anxieties are connected with one's physical health following a stroke or a heart operation. Of course a doctor's advice should be followed in this situation. The physical energy required for sexual activity has been compared to that required for climbing a flight of stairs or briskly walking two city blocks. If a husband has recovered sufficiently from a heart attack or a stroke to do these things comfortably, then it is usually safe for him to have sex. Reducing such anxiety allows for the *eros* love to be of a greater quality.

Since significant amounts of body energy are required for digestion after eating a large meal, it is strongly recommended that, especially for heart patients, sexual intercourse be avoided for at least two hours. Some say that there is a slight advantage to using the female-on-top position if the man has been the patient. The wife may be more protective and also more aggressive in this position during her husband's recuperation.[4]

Coach in the mind. Performance anxieties are common for men. The phrase, *sexual performance* con-

4. Wheat, *Intended for Pleasure*, p. 208.

jures up concepts of a stage, a pair of actors, and a room full of critics. In his own mind, a man with dominant performance anxieties stands back and watches his own performance, judging every aspect and comparing it to how he thinks good lovemaking should go. Masters and Johnson call this *preoccupation with self observation* or *spectatoring*. Lovemaking is not to be like a game that must be won or an event that must please some fans or a coach. The goal of lovemaking is simply to relax and enjoy being in close touch with each other. Instead of anxieties and pressures in marital love, there should be a sense of no demands. Relaxation means doing what you want to do when and how you decide to do it. There may be periods of aggressive effort, but the motivation comes from within and not, for example, from the coach in your mind who says he will drop you from the team or criticize you if you don't live up to his expectations.

Madonna complex. Another anxiety a man may have is called the madonna complex. He may view his wife as consistently right, so perfect, spiritual, intelligent, pure and holy, far above him, and hard to please, that he finally gives up trying to measure up to what he considers to be her level. He feels inferior and inadequate. His feelings toward her are mixed with admiration, resentment, guilt, and anxiety, especially in feeling sexually attracted or sexually inclined toward her. In such cases, the man usually needs to develop a better self-concept, but often the woman also needs to allow her human nature, struggles, and even her faults to be humbly shared with her husband. She needs to initiate sex at times, talk about what pleases her, and find areas of sex and even of life in general in which she can express admiration for and positive reinforcement for him.

Guilt

Another potential block to emotional intimacy is the emotion of guilt.

Sex Outside of Marriage

Sometimes unresolved issues go back to guilt feelings about premarital sex with each other. If so, these issues need to be discussed between the partners, apologies and confession need to be made, and forgiveness granted. Sometimes guilt feelings linger in the form of self-condemning messages about one's worth, even though various sins have been confessed. If this is the case, a Christian couple needs to accept God's forgiveness and then to *forgive themselves.* Their worth is based not on their spotless record but on the righteous position and unconditonal love and acceptance given by their loving, heavenly father.

False Guilt

Very often guilt that blocks emotional intimacy is false guilt—the feeling of anger at ourselves for breaking a manmade standard, one which really should have no authority over our lives. Sometimes counseling is needed to help an individual or a couple deal with feelings of guilt, especially if there has been incest, molestation, or rape in past years. A very good therapy for false guilt regarding marital sex is to read books and articles that discuss the subject. These may include Christian and non-Christian publications, as well as the Scriptures. The Song of Solomon contains one of the best descriptions of sex in marriage. Read these chapters together. Use a modern translation which gives a clearer version of the thoughts expressed by married lovers.

Very often adults carry false guilt about sex in the home. This guilt developed from the way sexual matters were handled when they were young. It is common, for instance, for children to repeat words they have heard from other children. When they are shamed for saying these words, negative standards regarding sex are being pressed into their minds. Sometimes parents give negative reactions to television programs or magazine pictures their children may have seen, ones that portray sex blatantly. Certainly moral values should be taught and the abuse of sex must be opposed. However, there must be a balance of positive information given to children about the beauties and goodness of sex as God originally designed it—*within marriage*. When children use unacceptable words that they have picked up from school or from neighborhood children, this becomes a key opportunity for parents to deal with the use of wrong words and to answer their questions, using positive teachings to clear up any misconceptions.[5]

5. Ibid., p. 230.

In counseling a couple who were now grandparents, a question was asked concerning their pattern of love and marital sex. The wife responded by saying, "Yes, we still do have sex, but we ask God to forgive us every time we do." She had false guilt that perhaps went all the way back to her childhood. God nowhere says that marital sex is wrong. In fact, it is his desire that married couples have a beautiful pattern of life in this area. The fact is, *we have God's permission to enjoy sex within marriage.* There is not to be any guilt feeling connected with sex in the context of a lifetime commitment. Rather, there is to be both a bodily and a spiritual union, and a growing knowledge of one another through the sexual relationship.

As mentioned previously, Scripture plainly warns that the husband and wife are not to defraud one another, that is, break up their normal pattern of sexual activity, unless this break is with *mutual consent.* And then it is to be for *a very limited time,* so that they may give themselves to prayer for some special burden they may have (1 Cor. 7:3–5).

In another counseling situation, I learned of a mother who told her daughter that, as far as sexual relations with her husband were concerned, she had endured them through the years and that was probably what the daughter should try to do also.

The net result of people who grow up in homes where they hear only negative comments concerning sex is that they see sex as something dirty, sinful, and of the devil, instead of something God invented. Christian parents must be very careful to maintain

God's viewpoint on sex in marriage, which is perhaps best summarized in Hebrews 13:4. "Let marriage be held in honor among all, and let the marriage bed be undefiled; for fornicators and adulterers God will judge." Our children need to hear these positive values that God himself teaches in Scripture, always placing sex in marriage in the light of perfect approval and yet separating it from sex outside of marriage.

Transference

Another possible block to emotional intimacy is that of transference, which can come in several forms.

Through an Affair

A primary transference has to do with a spouse's emotional investment in a person outside the marriage. This is sometimes called an emotional affair and often leads to a physical affair. The fine line between these two types of affairs gives sufficient grounds for being sensitive to keeping the marital relationship exclusive—*mutually* exclusive. Sometimes we hear statements such as, "Well, I can't talk to my spouse, and this third party (of the opposite sex, of course) is so supportive and understanding." This type of transference can result in an emotional divorce from one's spouse. Once a sufficient emotional investment has been made in a third party, the feelings of intimacy toward one's spouse may close off.

Through Past Issues

Transference can also be based on issues from the past. A spouse can transfer anger harbored toward another person by redirecting it toward his or her own mate. For example, if a husband has unresolved bitterness toward his mother or ex-spouse, he can develop this feeling toward his wife in what is sometimes called a *memory loop*. He blocks his other emotions toward her because he has not worked through to forgiveness the anger of the past issues.

Through Activities

A spouse can also transfer love for his mate to something that has become increasingly important to him, such as a job, a hobby, or a dream. This begins to show itself in an imbalance in lifestyle priorities. A mate may be so in love and involved with a job that it consumes most of his or her emotional energy. A woman's life may be wrapped around her children so that there is nothing left over for her husband. The primary excitement in one's life might be an addiction to golf, tennis, racquetball, baseball coaching, hunting, or even to an overbalance of church work. In this sense, an affair need not be just with another person but with anything that becomes more important to a person than a spouse.

Other Blocks

Other possible blocks to *eros* love could be the lack of functional spiritual life or satisfactory communication; unresolved problems in fulfilling practical responsibilities (such as repairing the dripping faucet or the sticking front door); poor perception of self-worth; power struggles, which can result when a wife rebels and will not yield to the husband's leadership role; and a lack of trust. Sometimes a block occurs when a woman becomes jealous of her own sexuality. In this regard, she assumes that her husband loves her only because of her capacity to provide him with sexual enjoyment. She looks at her sexual organs as she would a mistress. She feels she is only a sex object to her husband, used and invalued as an individual.

Components of Love

Love in a marital relationship is like an equilateral triangle, the sides of which are *eros* love, *phileo* love, and *agape* love. Each side is as important as the others.

Eros

Emotional love, the side of the triangle which is called *eros* love, needs to be nourished. Perhaps *eros* love is best described in Proverbs 5:18, 19 where the emotion and attraction toward the physical aspect of a lover's being is emphasized. *Eros* is the feeling side of love. It is a very important part of marriage even though it is a small part. When most people think and talk about love, they refer to this side of it--the physical attraction and sensual joy of *eros*. This side of love includes romantic marital sex. It is nurtured by hugs and touching, especially in nonsexual contacts. A couple would do well to examine this side of the love triangle in their marriage to see if it needs further nourishment. Many of the ideas suggested in this book will help.

Phileo

Phileo love, contrasted with *agape* love in John 21:16, is the second side of marital love's equilateral triangle. It is a relational love and involves having things in common, being best friends, dating, participating in hobbies or projects together, praying with one another, playing games together, going on vacations together, and having time in the schedule each week for relaxing and having fun. *Phileo* love, nurtured by communication, gives an optimal opportunity for each person in the marriage to reinvest his or her affection and reintroduces the courting and fun times somewhat similar to the couple's experiences when they first developed love and attraction for each other.

This friendship part of love stimulates the *eros* of love. Romance is really the combination of *eros* and *phileo*. Most women do not define romance as what happens in bed but what happens all day before the couple go to bed. In other words, romance is not *eros;* it is the corner of the triangle where *eros* and *phileo* meet. *Phileo* love delights in each other's presence with an underlying motivation to build each other's worth. How does this angle of your triangle look? Do the two sides of *phileo* and *eros* fail to meet because of wrong priorities and a lack of time? What further steps can you take to develop a *phileo* that will yield a more complete, healthy *eros* between the two of you?

Agape

The third side of the love triangle is *agape* love, mentioned in Ephesians 5:25 and many other places in the New Testament. It is not necessarily connected to feelings but to a love that chooses. *Agape* love involves commitment and taking the initiative to meet the needs in another's life, resulting in his or her growth and spiritual maturity. This love is nurtured by the spiritual life of the couple as their commitment to God remains strong, as their growth in his Word continues to develop, and as their commitment to each other continues to receive strength. This commitment enables them to work out their problems in any of the other areas of their life without giving up the marriage. If there are some problems with *eros*, *agape* love revitalizes it by establishing the commitment to talk about these issues and to work them out. *Agape* love also gives momentum to projects, which develops *phileo* love. It *chooses* to meet true needs and helps a couple to reevaluate priorities.

Revitalizing Emotional Love

Two ways for helping a couple revitalize real love and its associated emotions are to adjust behavior and thinking. Since we can't command our emotions directly, we can affect them indirectly by *choosing* our behavior and *choosing* what we think.

Changing Behavior

The behavior approach to love is illustrated in Revelation 2:4, 5, where the Lord Jesus Christ gave instructions to John for the church at Ephesus in how to regain its lost love. They were based on a behavioral model. The Christians at Ephesus were to "*do the first works*"—what they did when they first became Christians. This meant getting back to those exciting activities that characterize young Christians.

Often we will have a young couple map out ideas on how they would care for and act toward each other if they still had their strong honeymoon-type of love. After making a commitment to act on that set of ideas toward each other, they come back the following week, often saying that their feelings of love have been reignited. Of course, there are many other behaviors that needed to be added to that, such as practicing expressions of love, like those given in 1 Corinthians 13:4–8—the Bible's "love chapter"—and other important Scriptures.

Changing Thinking

To readjust thinking, we often have an individual or even the couple commit themselves to writing five positive qualities of his or her spouse on a 3 × 5 card and to spending ten minutes daily meditating on those, while rigorously challenging any negative thoughts about the spouse that might come to mind. Such meditation may include some key sections of the Song of Solomon that apply to their marriage situation.

Changing Prayers

Thinking and feelings also can be helped by praying and then acting in faith. Claiming God's love instead of depending primarily on one's own can be expressed in a prayer like the following.

Dear Lord, I confess that I do not have the love I should have for my spouse. Thank you that you love my spouse and that you live within me. I claim by faith the release of your love through me to my spouse. And I now choose to act on my belief in your love. Thank you for that love. I pray in Jesus' name. Amen.

When thinking and praying in faith are translated into action, we have found that the feelings desired to renew emotional intimacy in Christian marriage will begin to reappear.

4

Three Phases
of Romantic Sex

The three general phases of romantic sex are *foreplay, intercourse,* and *afterglow.* Some would mistakenly suggest that foreplay and afterglow are what happen before and after the "real thing." However, all three phases *are* the real thing. All three make up the entire picture.

Foreplay

Foreplay is very important in romantic sex. Strangely, though, this is the ingredient that is often missing. In some cases, the husband sees it as a chore, because he has not learned the techniques of foreplay, or perhaps because he has not understood why it might be so important to his wife.

Foreplay is like turning on a mental switch. It is getting the thoughts moving in the right erotic direction. When a husband jumps right into intercourse without preparing his wife and considering her needs, she may feel that she is being used, or that the husband is simply thinking of his own needs. He needs to be emotionally involved and to show concern, tenderness, and love before, as well as during, the actual intercourse.

It is important to understand the two parts that must be addressed in foreplay. These are *seduction* and *arousal*.

Seduction

The mind is involved in seduction. Both husband and wife need to be mentally ready for romantic love. Both must become mentally and emotionally ready to enjoy it with eagerness.

Arousal

The body is concerned with arousal. This is the physical preparation. The wife needs to be brought to a state of preparation for intercourse, whereas a man usually gets into the mood by visual foreplay. He is turned on by his wife's body—her face, her breasts, her legs.

Foreplay accomplishes both emotional and physical preparation. This is especially important to the wife, since she needs more time to reach orgasm. The husband needs to realize that he must give her pleasure for a while without expecting anything specific

Sexual Response Pattern

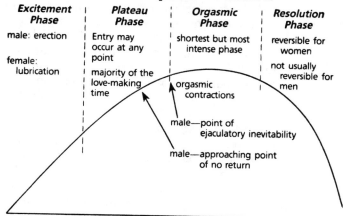

Excitement Phase	Plateau Phase	Orgasmic Phase	Resolution Phase
male: erection	Entry may occur at any point	shortest but most intense phase	reversible for women
female: lubrication	majority of the love-making time		not usually reversible for men

orgasmic contractions

male—point of ejaculatory inevitability

male—approaching point of no return

Adapted from Masters and Johnson, *Human Sexual Response* (Boston: Little, Brown, & Co 1966).

in return. In that way, she can get a head start down her longer road toward orgasm.

Feelings that should be transmitted during foreplay include gentleness, tenderness, love, excitement, passion, and enthusiasm—not crudeness, rudeness, or impatience!

Ten Parts of Foreplay

Generally, foreplay includes touching, intimate talk, kissing, hugging, petting, cuddling, massaging, and stimulation.

1. *Relaxing.* Foreplay helps the couple to unwind after a busy day. It can begin by snuggling

close to each other and slowly stepping out of the daily routine with a new focus on each other. As they snuggle and cuddle, a couple can relax the tensions of the day by relaxing their muscles and rubbing each other in sore areas, simply for the purpose of releasing tension.

Some couples enjoy relaxing by bathing or showering together or soaking in a hot tub. As mentioned earlier, this not only provides delight in lovemaking but cleanliness shows respect to the other partner and an anticipation for closeness. What better time to take a shower or bath than when you expect intimacy?

2. *Kissing.* This is another essential part of foreplay. If the husband takes the time to make kissing enjoyable, it makes his wife sense an emotional warmth and helps her to know that their romantic experience will be very good. Some would suggest that kissing can be progressive. The first step may be that of closed lips with kisses that are warm and soft. The next step would be a little more passionate type of kissing with the lips a little more firm. This stage can sometimes be the type that encourages the partner's lips to open to enjoy exploring each other's mouths with their tongues, a little bit of French kissing.[1] Of course, kissing does not have to be limited to the face. Kisses anywhere on the body can excite the wife and arouse her emotions.

1. Morgenstern, *How to Make Love*, p. 68.

3. *Undressing* each other as a part of foreplay can be seductive and arousing. Be creative and approach this slowly.
4. *Verbal communication.* An essential part of lovemaking is communication. Women like intimate talk during romantic sex. The wife needs to hear that her husband appreciates her, and he also needs to hear the same from her. Share what feels good and provide instructions, "I prefer this," or "A little to the right," or "That feels good," especially if the partner asks. Be encouraging, not demanding.
5. *Total body caressing.* This can be very enjoyable for both in foreplay. There is hardly a square inch that isn't a trigger to sexual arousal for the woman, if the mood is right and the touch is one that expresses caring.
6. *Massaging.* Closely related to caressing is massaging. It is an important part of lovemaking as well. Lubricants can increase the skin's sensitivity during massaging. These include scented massage oils, mineral oils, body lotions, jells, or even ordinary vegetable oil. Such lubricants can add much to the enjoyment and may be purchased at drugstores or specialty shops.

   Even massaging can be progressive in its stages, beginning with the nonerogenous parts, such as the back of the neck, the small of the back, the calves, the stomach, the inside of the knees, and the inner thighs, and then on to the erogenous zones, especially the breasts and the nipples. The husband and wife can both participate in massaging.

7. *Petting.* It may be just another way of looking at massaging or cuddling but with more intensity. It is not only important in foreplay but during actual intercourse as well. Petting and fondling should be gentle. Some women complain that their husbands squeeze too hard or grab their breasts in a way that does not feel good.[2] Most women do not like to have their nipples nipped at by their husbands.[3]

8. *Stimulation of the wife's clitoris.* This is a very important part of foreplay. Some call the clitoris the woman's *love button.* It is the place of greatest nerve concentration and sexual pleasure on the woman's body, and it contains as many nerve endings as the head of the man's penis.

Most women require the stimulation of the clitoris in order to achieve orgasm. Since it is the most sensitive part of the vagina, the husband should probably begin by rubbing the inner lips on either side of the clitoris and then continue by making circular motions around it rather than by pushing on it too hard or too directly. He can ask directions from his wife as he fondles her.

If a man has trouble finding the clitoris, his best approach would be to ask his wife to help

2. Ibid., p. 72.
3. Crenshaw, *Bedside Manners*, p. 180.

him. Technically, the clitoris is located at the top of the minor lips. The top of the lips join in a V and blend right into the head of the clitoris.[4] The clitoris swells when aroused and feels like a small nipple or bump at the top or head of the vagina.

9. *Mutual stimulation.* This can also be a part of foreplay. It is not just the contact of the genitals that are involved here, but the entire body. The entire body is to be given over to the other partner for romantic love.

10. *Fresh ideas.* Very important from time to time in foreplay is the introduction of new ideas and techniques. One of the best ways to keep that freshness is to explore new sexual possibilities. There needs to be, however, not only freedom but mutual consent to all ideas. One couple's new idea, for instance, was to use whipped cream on various erotic places on the body. Let your imagination be creative.

The people of our generation who have no moral values change sexual partners when things get boring. But we who have accepted Christ as our Savior should instead keep creative ideas flowing and change what we do with our partners, rather than considering the world's option of changing partners.

In our thoughts about foreplay, we should add the fact that foreplay need not always be as complex as all of the ideas we have suggested so far in this sec-

4. Ibid., p. 178.

tion, but certainly combinations of these ideas add a great deal of zest and meaning to romantic sex.

Intercourse

The second general area of romantic sex is *intercourse*. Since this book is written for couples who have been married for a number of years, it is not our intent to go into actual basics, which we assume the readers have studied well. Many good books that give descriptions of the basics of intercourse can be purchased. Basically we want to give some information about the importance of trying a variety of positions, since we feel it is essential to have freshness and creativity in the sexual relationship. We find a good percentage of couples have never tried any position other than the standard man-on-top position, which can certainly contribute to boredom.

Basic Positions

There are many varieties that can develop out of the basic positions we are mentioning here. The common position is face-to-face with the man-on-top. A couple may want to start with this position, but, in order to delay the husband's climax, shift to other positions as intercourse progresses and finally, end with the man-on-top position again as the one most likely to produce mutual orgasm.

The second basic position from which many other positions can be derived is the *woman-on-top* position. This leaves the woman astride and free to control length and intensity of intercourse. She can shift to lying, kneeling, or other positions without losing contact. Some specialists say that the *woman-astride* gives the greatest pleasure for both partners. At least 75 percent of all Americans now turn to the woman-on-top position at least some of the time. A recent study by a Chicago-based sex therapist notes that a majority of both men and women find the woman-on-top position more sexually exciting than the missionary position.[5] This position has additional benefits in that it allows the woman to determine the rhythm of the lovemaking, which can make a very important difference to her. It also frees the husband's hands to caress her breasts and other parts of her body. It allows better clitoral stimulation during intercourse, not only from the natural context but through manual stimulation. This is a better position if the man weighs a great deal more than the woman.[6]

The third basic position from which a variety of other subpositions are derived is called the *rear-entry* position. In this position, both partners can be either lying or kneeling, or in various sitting postures.

During intercourse, it is important that some form of lubricant be applied to avoid any pain. Sometimes a wife does not produce enough natural lubricant. There are a number of good ones on the market that can be purchased at almost any drugstore for lubricating the clitoris, vaginal opening, and head of the penis.

Afterglow

The third phase in romantic sex is *afterglow*. The afterglow is as much a part of lovemaking as are

5. Morgenstern, *How to Make Love*, p. 95.
6. Ibid., p. 94.

foreplay and intercourse. It is difficult for a husband
to understand the importance of this third phase if
he does not communicate well with his wife in order
to get her feedback on this phase.

Afterglow is a time of cuddling, holding, and support through words of appreciation and reaffirma-
tion. If they don't have this, women will sometimes
have a feeling of loneliness immediately after orgasm. It is devastating to a wife to have her husband
turn his back on her and forget about her immediately after orgasm. She sometimes sees it as a form
of rejection.

This phase of afterglow may take as long as fifteen
minutes before all the physical signs of arousal are
gone.[7] This phase insures a complete transition to
relaxation together.

7. Wheat, *Intended for Pleasure*, p. 88.

5

Wives and Orgasm

Many women are not sure whether or not they have experienced orgasm. They may know what makes them feel comfortable in romantic sex, but they are not sure about experiencing orgasm.

According to the Hite Report, only 52 percent of sexually active women in the United States have orgasm on a regular or even occasional basis.[1] But most women are fully capable of experiencing orgasm. In fact, some can have one orgasm after another. A woman may prefer not to have an orgasm with every sexual experience; at other times she may want several.

Another interesting fact is that it takes much longer for the average woman to reach an orgasm than a man, perhaps from seven to ten minutes.

1. Morgenstern, *How to Make Love*, p. 102.

What Is an Orgasm?

In both men *and* women, orgasm involves a series of quick rhythmic-like muscle contractions throughout the pelvic region that last for a few seconds.[2] In men, orgasm usually has two phases. First, there is a convulsive reaction from the entire body. The second phase is the ejaculation. While these usually occur simultaneously, it is true that each can occur without the other.

In a woman, orgasm consists of two phases, also. First, there is an involuntary, convulsive reaction similar to a man's contractions. This involves the muscle surrounding the vagina called the P.C. (pubococcygeus) muscle. At this time the blood begins to accumulate in the pelvic area, the vagina begins to lubricate the outer lips and the inner lips, and the clitoris enlarges. The nipples stiffen and the darker skin around the nipples begins to swell. Then the vagina contracts. Breathing speeds up, blood pressure rises, and the pulse increases. At this peak, orgasm occurs. The muscular tension reaches a peak. The outer third of the vagina contracts rhythmically about every second for a brief time. Then a warm feeling usually flows throughout the body as the blood that has rushed into the pelvic area is released.[3]

What Interferes with Reaching Orgasm?

Five Hindrances

Orgasm is hampered, first, *by the inability to get the mind to think sexual thoughts.* Much of sexual

2. Castleman, *Sexual Solutions*, p. 152.
3. Morgenstern, *How to Make Love*, pp. 106–107.

enjoyment is mental. The woman, especially, needs to be thinking sexual thoughts. Otherwise, orgasm is extremely unlikely.

Second, *anxieties and fears* can hinder reaching orgasm. A great deal of psychological study has confirmed that anxiety and fear, more than any other factor, keep a woman from having orgasm. Any kind of fear or anxiety can bring an end to the enjoyment of romantic sex. Perhaps the greatest fear is the fear of not performing. This may be the reason why most men and women lose their ability to perform sexually—because they want so desperately to do so.

Third, many times *the husband does not take enough time preparing the wife.* The woman needs to be relaxed in order to come to orgasm, and this is impossible unless the husband takes sufficient time with foreplay and physical intimacy.

Fourth, *lack of communication* is a hindrance. If the husband is not sure his wife reaches orgasm or wants to reach orgasm, he should discuss this with her.

Fifth, *ignorance* can be a hindrance. The wife who has never experienced orgasm needs to get more in touch with her body. Discovering and becoming familiar with her own body is essential for her to be able to communicate to her husband. Counselors advise that a woman become familiar with herself by touching various points around and on the clitoris to learn where the best feelings occur for her. Being knowledgeable as to where the pleasure points are and where she may experience pain is important so that she can communicate these to her husband, and thus achieve the fullest enjoyment and orgasm.

Becoming Orgasmic

Almost any woman can learn to become orgasmic. Besides knowing her own body, this learning process includes learning to relax; learning to focus on arousal; and extending sensuality, stimulation, and intimate conversation about pleasurable preferences. Both parties need to make romantic sex fun and have a sense of humor connected with it.

How to Reach an Orgasm

Importance of Time

Time should be given to relax and express affection when trying to achieve orgasm. Spend as much time as possible in foreplay. Again, the mental goal should be to enjoy one another. For most women, clitoral stimulation is essential to reach orgasm. Many women are not able to be orgasmic with only thrusting in intercourse. While manual stimulation is appropriate whenever it feels good, during thrusting it can be distracting for the woman as well as uncomfortable for the man. As said before, some women feel it is easier for them to reach orgasm during the woman-on-top position.

Mutual Orgasm

If the husband and wife do not reach orgasm together, then what? While it is possible that they can reach climax and orgasm at the same time, it is not necessary for them to do so. They should, however, enjoy their own orgasm. All the while the mental attitude must be playful. Don't work at it too hard. Make it fun and enjoyable.

6

Husbands and Erection

What Is Impotence?

Impotence is the failure to achieve or maintain an erection for sexual intercourse. Someone has defined impotence as a penis in rebellion.[1] While impotence is the usual word to describe this problem, it perhaps is not the best. Impotence suggests a lack of power, but usually that is not the problem. In reality, impotence is an inability to get the power to the penis.

Extent and Effects

The extent of impotence is rather surprising. When a man one day faces up to the fact that he is having a problem, he usually feels he is one of the very few men in the world with that problem. However, most

1. Reuben, *How to Get More*, p. 126.

men, at some time or another, lose an erection during intercourse. For some men it is just an occasional occurrence. But for others it is a seemingly insurmountable difficulty. A conservative estimate is that ten million men in the United States have erection problems.[2]

The effects of impotence can be emotionally devastating to the man who experiences it. Impotence can cause depression and suicidal tendencies if not resolved. Because of its potentially devastating emotional impact, a person needs to know how to handle it.

This is how impotence can come about. Theresa Larsen Crenshaw points out in her book, *Bedside Manners:*

You have two nervous systems. One is under voluntary control. That's the one that says, "move, arm" or "close, eyes," or "walk," and your arm moves, your eyes close, you walk. You have very good control over that.

The other system is involuntary (automatic). It is in charge of running your body, whether you are paying attention or not. It makes you breathe whether you are thinking about it or not. It controls your heart rate, the size of your pupils, blood flow to the intestinal tract, blood flow to the skin and other organs. Most of us have very little control over this nervous system.

The autonomic system is divided into two portions—the *sympathetic* and the *parasympathetic.* These two systems do opposite things to your body.

2. Crenshaw, *Bedside Manners*, p. 188.

The sympathetic system is very easy to remember because it is in charge when you need action; the flight, fight, and fear response. The parasympathetic system is in charge when your body is calm. . . . the last thing you need is blood flow to your skin if you're going to fight—you would bleed more. If you're going to flee, you need that blood in your leg muscles instead. . . . your cardiovascular system considers your penis a superficial skin structure. The vessels respond to the sympathetic system and constrict. The erection is lost almost immediately.

Loss of erection actually results from a chemical within your body triggered by fear. An emotion (fear) causes a chemical (adrenalin) to instantly appear in your bloodstream. The mind causes chemical and physical reactions in the body.

Adrenalin causes specific physical reactions within the body. It causes impotence by directly constricting the blood vessels in your penis—just as it does those in your skin—and the erection is lost. The more upset you get about it, the more adrenalin pumps into your system, and the more impossible it is to become erect again.

. . . A major cause of psychological impotence is fear of performance. A man who is worried whether or not he is going to get erect . . . is pumping adrenalin into his system. . . . He discovers that he cannot will an erection, and begins to suspect that something is physically wrong with him.[3]

Contributing Factors to Impotence

Let us look at some contributing factors to the problem of impotence.

3. Ibid., pp. 183–86.

1. Boredom can be a big factor. After a couple has been married a number of years, a man may begin to complain about doing the same old thing in the same old way. There needs to be freshness in the love life.
2. Loss of concentration and feelings can cause some impotence problems. Impotence may be the man's penis saying to him, "Listen to what I am telling you."[4] It could be telling the man that his subconscious mind is not being fed the proper erotic thoughts about his wife.
3. Fatigue becomes more of a concern as a man reaches middle age.
4. Depression is a reaction to some loss of self-esteem, a personal goal, a possession, or other disappointment.
5. Stress is change or challenge that sends excess adrenalin into the system.
6. Anxiety distracts the normal mental focus.
7. Anger and resentment can make the penis pout.
8. Environmental factors such as temperature, other persons in the house, or an uncomfortable place or surroundings can cause impotence.
9. Being pressed for time contributes. One source indicates that healthy seventy-year-olds have intercourse approximately twice a week while thirty-year-olds average once a week. The reason for the difference is that the thirty-year-olds are out in the world, driving hard to make

4. Ibid., p. 202.

a living, feeling uptight about being angry with their wives, and having all the other difficulties of living together, raising children, and always being in a hurry. At seventy, there is time for each other and, assuming both are healthy, time to enjoy sex.[5]

10. Drugs, alcohol, and smoking can contribute to impotence.

11. Some chemicals that are used to fatten livestock can have an effect on men, especially those over the age of forty. It is suggested that a man who has reached middle age eat less red meat and more fish and poultry.

12. Certain medications can definitely contribute to impotency.

13. Illnesses contribute to the problem. Some stress-related illnesses are high blood pressure, ulcers, colitis, and heart disease. Any illness from flu to cancer can decrease interest in lovemaking and indirectly in an erection. Decreased sexual interest is the body's way of investing its energy in the task of restoring its health.

Some men with diabetes develop erection problems. Kidney dialysis may cause erection problems. The building of fatty plaque in the artery walls may impair erection to a degree. Sickle cell anemia, a disease that affects mainly black people, may affect occasional blocking of the blood flow to the penis. Heart disease,

5. Ibid., pp.195–96.

on the other hand, need not affect a man's erective ability. The removal of the prostate gland usually leaves most but not all men nonerective, because of the effect on the lower spinal nerves. Any other injury to the nerves in the lower spine may decrease the capacity for erection.

14. The wrong mental image of one's wife can affect a man's performance. The wife's growing older may enhance a view of her as a mature, motherly person. A significant sign of an excessive tendency to see one's wife as his mother is a decrease in sexual interest in her.[6] The way a wife talks to her husband may set up resentment in him or hurt his ego, and cause him to see her in a motherly role. If the wife is a dominant individual, and if the husband does not accept that, he may develop a complete lack of interest as a way of retaliating. He may do this in a conscious or malicious way, or he may do it unconsciously, as his anger seeks an outlet.

15. Lack of good communication has an adverse effect on lovemaking. Impotence may be a sign that one partner has lost interest in relating meaningfully to the other. It may even reflect a wish to fail that comes from one or the other no longer loving or caring for a mate.

6. Jacobs, *Overcoming Impotence*, p. 19.

Some Solutions to Erection Problems

When to See a Doctor

All erection problems should start with a good look at one's own life, a man's feelings about himself, and the kinds of relationships that he experiences. The chances are that a man does not need to visit a doctor because of his impotency if he can produce an erection by direct stimulation, or if he finds that he does become erect during the night during "dreams." This is an indication that he, in fact, can become erect and that there is some psychological factor to be reckoned with. A visit to the doctor is in order if he cannot reach an erection at all, or if his problem is becoming increasingly worse, or if he wants to rule out potentially organic factors.

A man with impotence problems needs his wife to be on his team and not against him.[7] He needs a wife who is compassionate, patient, and understanding while he works on a solution.

Physical Intimacy Is Important

Some men, because of their impotence problems, no longer attempt to hold, cuddle, caress, or try any alternative form of sexual activity with their wives. They deprive themselves of physical intimacy by choice, not by circumstance. In fact, just seeking to enjoy cuddling, caressing, and holding, without any

7. Reuben, *How to Get More*, p. 156.

plans of intercourse, may bring about the erection that he cannot command by his will.

As a couple gets older, prime time should be given to romantic sex. There is usually a narrower time span for them both to be sexually responsive. It is not only prime time that is important, but the assurance of privacy, during which the couple can be together and communicate in an unhurried fashion without concern of being disturbed. There is usually a need for more direct genital stimulation as the male enters his midforties.[8] This is important, since stimulation from his wife as a sexual partner complements the need because his brain has become less willing to provide its own particular brand of erotic electricity.[9]

Make Necessary Changes

The couple should change their sleeping habits, if need be, with the development of more sexual closeness as well as personal intimacy. This could increase for both if they start to sleep in the nude (in the same bed, of course). There needs to be the reestablishment of intimacy in lovemaking. It may be good to postpone intercourse for a while and focus on the nongenital ways of feeling aroused. The wife probably knows that her fondling of her husband's penis gives him pleasure. The husband should let her know what else turns him on. As he shares with her, she probably will have some secrets to share with him for his consideration.

8. Jacobs, *Overcoming Impotence*, pp. 32, 38.
9. Reuben, *How to Get More*, p. 134.

If a man is impotent for physical reasons, he should not despair. There are effective treatments even in these cases. There is no cause for any man to remain impotent for any reason, unless health or choice precludes surgery.[10] Your doctor will advise you if implant surgery is an option, but this should be considered only as a last resort.[11]

Exercise for Regaining Erection

Reverse Psychology

Some experts suggest that the best cure for impotency is to go to bed consciously rejecting the possibility of having an erection and engaging in intercourse. This reverse psychology seems to build up desire and capability. In this process, anything is okay (such as petting, hugging, and kissing), except trying to become erect. If you do gain an erection, do not try to do anything about it. The main thing is to focus on pleasure. Don't worry when you begin to lose an erection. It will come back, if not that night, then the next time.

A number of therapists recommend a three-week recovery program for impotency problems.

Week 1.   The couple should sleep together and engage in cuddling, hugging, kissing, and caressing, but without touching the genital areas or the wife's breasts, and with-

10. Crenshaw, *Bedside Manners*, p. 204.
11. Castelman, *Sexual Solutions*, p. 131.

out having intercourse. Time should be set aside each night for this. The time could be split between the husband caressing the wife, and after that, each of them giving the other a body massage. The massaging should have the touch of a caress with a feeling of care.[12] During this process a stronger feeling of closeness with each other should develop.

Week 2. Included with the caressing and massaging, in the second week comes the new liberty of massaging the genitals and breasts. If the husband's arousal builds tension, that is fine. But there still should be no intercourse during this second week.

Week 3. This week should include caressing with love, with no definite plan for intercourse. If it happens during this week, it happens. During this week of manual stimulation of each other, the couple should be creative, but they should touch the erogenous areas only after spending some time in general body caressing.

The woman-on-top position is perhaps the easiest for rebuilding the enjoyment of intercourse for this type of procedure. When having renewed sexual intercourse, after these weeks of relating to one another in this new way, there should not be any burden or pressure to try to achieve

---

12. Jacobs, *Overcoming Impotence*, pp. 66–67.

the ideal of simultaneous climaxes.[13] Such a goal builds anxiety and puts a performance factor into the equation that is not necessary at this time.

Dr. Wheat emphasizes the role of the wife as one of holding the key to the cure for her husband. Unfortunately, women who complain the most about their husbands not being able to satisfy them sexually are often the ones who are the least cooperative when it it comes to working the problem out together.

Dr. Wheat points out that according to secular therapists, the rate of cure of impotence is 50 to 75 percent. However, he observes "a rate of cure which is much higher for the Christian husband who claims and uses his extra resource against the main villain—*fear* of failure. God has given us resources far greater than the spirit of fear, and resting in that knowledge will provide the Christian husband with a stability and relaxation that can go far in solving almost every impotency problem."[14]

For God has not given us a spirit of timidity, but of power and love and self-discipline (2 Tim. 1:7).

---

13. Ibid., p. 74.
14. Wheat, *Intended for Pleasure*, pp. 127–29.

7

Husbands' Problem Plaguers

Premature Ejaculation

A British study showed that the common obstacle in sexual enjoyment is the woman's frustration caused by a man who ejaculates before she is sexually satisfied. An American survey also showed that three-fourths of men ejaculate less than two minutes after inserting the penis into the vagina.[1] Early ejaculation is especially common with men new to sexual intercourse. The essence of the problem is that most women take longer to reach orgasm than men. Of course, the husband can stimulate the wife's clitoris after he himself has climaxed, but romantic sex will

---

1. Diagram Group, *User's Manual*, p. 142.

be far more pleasurable for both if the husband can learn to maintain an erection as long as possible. (An occasional premature ejaculation occurs even in the experience of those men who have developed a general pattern of control. This happens especially when there has been an absence of intercourse for a number of days.)

A problem that sometimes emerges in connection with premature ejaculation is that after his orgasm, a satisfied husband has a tendency to discontinue his physical attention to his wife and thus disregards her unfulfilled needs.[2]

In discovering the solution to the problem, the first and most important factor is a cooperative and caring wife. Fortunately, premature ejaculation is easy to treat. Let us share a variety of approaches.

1. A very simple experiment is to try to reduce the tension that the husband may be experiencing. If he lies beneath his wife, taking a fairly inactive role, he will experience less muscular tension and therefore may be less likely to ejaculate prematurely.[3]
2. Another approach to the solution is called the "squeeze technique." It can be accomplished by the man himself or as a second approach, by his wife. If a man is about to ejaculate, he can usually stop it by pressing his own thumb against the frenum, that is, the sensitive under-

2. Wheat, *Intended for Pleasure*, p. 91.
3. Diagram Group, *User's Manual*, p. 142.

side of the penis where the glans or head meets the shaft. He may need one or two fingers on the underside for leverage, but all he needs to do is squeeze just a little—not too hard—and hold it for a few seconds.[4] Then he can continue his intercourse until he comes near the point of ejaculation again when he can follow the same method once more. This procedure can build up his endurance time.

The alternative is to have his wife squeeze his penis with her thumb and forefinger. Once he feels some distance from his point of no return, his wife can stop the squeezing, and they can return to their intercourse.

3. If a man is very sensitive, these first two methods may not work. Such an extrasensitive man needs to learn to appreciate physical closeness with his wife without ejaculation. They should spend several periods the first week doing those things that physically please each other, such as massaging, while avoiding stimulation of the genital areas. There must be no intercourse during this type of therapy. The next week, spend several periods that add the direct stimulation of the genital areas. As the wife manually stimulates her husband's penis, he signals when he feels an orgasm coming. She then stops stroking the penis and begins squeezing it below the rim of the glans. This procedure makes his erection subside. This is repeated several times, until fi-

4. Morgenstern, *How to Make Love*, p. 158.

nally she allows ejaculation to occur.[5] The third week, after sufficient foreplay, the couple can begin to engage in sexual intercourse. As they do, when he feels he is coming close to the point of no return, he withdraws the penis, and she squeezes it until he loses his erection. This can be repeated several times until the man is able to build up tolerance and control over his endurance.

Prostate Gland Problems

Another problem that must be addressed is the prostate-gland problem. A healthy prostate gland is essential to problem-free romantic love and for general well-being. Cancer of the prostate gland is the third most common form of malignancy among North American males—the third greatest cause of death by cancer.

Early Detection

One of the major problems in prostatic cancer is the fact that it is difficult to detect in its early stages. Examination must depend on manipulation by the physician's fingers to feel the surface of the gland for any disturbing growths, and these can exist long before any alarming symptoms are detected.[6]

The *Saturday Evening Post*, October 1983, published an article titled "Prostate Cancer, A National

5. Dunbar, *A Man's Sexual Health*, p. 113.
6. Ibid., p. 76.

Tragedy," by Cory Ser Vass, M.D. The American Cancer Society predicted then that twenty-four thousand men would die of advanced prostate cancer that year. Since black males have twice the incidence of prostatic cancer as white males, it is even more important for them to have an examination annually. In fact, a digital prostate gland examination should be part of a regular medical check-up for any man over forty years of age. Studies have shown that cancer of the prostate occurs in a significant percentage of men who eat a diet high in fat and protein content. A lower incidence of cancer of the prostate has been found in men who regularly eat higher amounts of vitamin A and green and yellow vegetables.[7] The most important point to remember about cancer of the prostate is that it is fairly easily detected by your physician's examination. When detected early, the outlook for this disease is very good, but advanced cases are much more difficult for a doctor to control.

Symptoms

It has been estimated that 60 percent of men over the age of sixty have some enlargement of the prostate gland. By the age of eighty, the estimate climbs to an estimated 95 percent. If it is a simple or benign enlargement, there may be no noticeable symptoms other than a slowing of the stream during urination. If inflammation of the gland is involved, then this can cause pain and difficulties when urinating. This

7. Cory Ser Vass, "Prostate Cancer, A National Tragedy," *The Saturday Evening Post* 255 (October 1983):26, 28.

problem can usually be controlled or cured through the use of antibiotic drugs.

Another symptom is the increased frequency of urination, which may be caused by a blockage or narrowing that the prostate gland produces in the urethra and neck of the bladder. If a man cannot empty his bladder, a buildup of fluid in the bladder may result, which can cause infection of that organ. This can also cause increased pressure on the kidneys through backup of urine, further aggravating the problem of infection.[8]

The Best Defense

One of the best ways to avoid problems that cause enlargement of the prostate is to have sex regularly. Each time a man has sexual intercourse, the prostate vigorously contracts and efficiently massages itself. A regular pattern of intercourse is the best defense against enlargement of the prostate.

When a man ejaculates, the prostate secretes most of the fluid that is expelled from the body. In a healthy man, the prostate gland will continue to function most of his life. If the prostate gland becomes infected, the urine may contain pus or a small amount of blood and be discolored. Any symptoms that indicate infection or inflammation should signal a man to consult his physician as soon as possible.

Prostatitis

Enlargement of the prostate itself does not cause or contribute to impotence or premature ejaculation,

8. Dunbar, *A Man's Sexual Health*, p. 74.

and it has virtually no effect on normal intercourse. If, however, there are repeated episodes of failure to ejaculate, especially following prolonged arousal periods, there may well be some reason to consider the possibility of a condition of the prostate known as *prostatitis*.[9] If at all possible, a regular pattern of sexual intercourse is a positive help in preventing prostate troubles.

The Creator gave us sex for our enjoyment. If you experience any of the problems mentioned in these chapters, realize that was *not* a part of God's plan for your happiness. Seek your physician's advice and medical knowledge. Grow closer to your wife in romantic love.

9. Wheat, *Intended for Pleasure*, p. 74.

8

Wives' Problem Plaguers

Painful Intercourse

Intercourse should be painless. If there is pain during intercourse, that pain is the body communicating that something is wrong somewhere. Many times pain and irritation during intercourse is simply from a lack of generous amounts of lubrication. Artificial lubricants, such as K-Y Jelly, can be easily purchased at any drugstore.

However, when pain persists even with plenty of lubrication, then consult a doctor to determine if there is a medical problem. Different types of pain may indicate trouble in different areas of the woman's body.

Vaginal Pain

Most commonly, vaginal pain results from infections in the vagina, and one symptom is a discharge.

A small amount of vaginal discharge is normal for any woman. Some women emit more than others. These normal secretions are white and there is no odor or itching. Abnormal or odorous discharge, itching, burning, or irritation may be body signs indicating yeast infections or vaginitis. Diagnosis and treatment by a physician should occur with these symptoms. A small infection left unchecked can move to other reproductive organs or to the bladder or kidneys.

Clitoral Pain

Though there occasionally may be a medical reason for clitoral pain, the most common reason would be lack of tenderness on the part of the husband during clitoral stimulation.

Unfortunately, a man by his own experience cannot know where the clitoris is located. All he knows is what he has learned from books and seen in diagrams and, if fortunate, learned from his wife. Although he may have read about some "foolproof" way to locate the clitoris, he still may never know if he is on target, or how hard he is rubbing, unless his wife has learned the secret of communicating and gently guiding his hand to help him know what gives her pleasure.

Cervical Pain

Cervicitis is an infection of the neck of the womb and is quite common. If there is cervical or uterine pain during intercourse, especially noticeable during deep thrusting, this may indicate an infection, if lubrication does not relieve it. *Endometriosis* occurs when small bits of tissue of the uterus lining migrate to other parts of the body. This causes fibrous growths and possibly inflammation in the uterus, the fallopian tubes, or the ovaries. Intermittent pain would be most noticeable with deep thrusting.

Other Discomforts

Constipation could cause pain with deep thrusting and would be uncomfortable. Proper nutrition is the key to this problem.

Some women may experience bladder pressure or discomfort due to a uterus that is not properly positioned due to weakened ligaments. Emptying the bladder before intercourse will help to alleviate such pressure.

Kidney and bladder infections could cause pain as well and a visit to the doctor's office is a "must" in these cases.

It is true that many diseases are emotionally induced. Doctors in years past have passed off painful intercourse problems as being just stress-induced or psychological. If you are not satisfied with a first doctor's opinion or the results of his or her treatment, go to a second or more until you get a solution. Don't just grin and bear it. Prolonged pain during intercourse can lead to stress and possibly other psychological problems.

Some safeguards against vaginal infections:

1. After urination or bowel movements, cleanse from front to back with toilet paper. Yeasts nor-

mally live in the rectum and intestinal tract.
They can enter the vagina if the rectum is wiped
first and the paper touches the vagina as it is
moved to the bladder opening.

2. Wear panties with cotton crotches, since nylon
does not absorb moisture. Yeasts thrive in warm,
moist conditions.

3. An occasional douche will not hurt the vagina,
and perhaps should be used after a menstrual
period or if there is some vaginal discharge. Use
a mild aromatic powder or liquid available at
drug stores.

Menopause

A great concern of many women is that menopause
will affect their sex life. Some women think they will
lose interest in and no longer enjoy the pleasures of
marital sex. Some fear they will lose their femininity
and thus their sex appeal, so that their husbands will
no longer love them. These are false concerns.

Definition

Menopause, simply put, is a woman's monthly
menstrual cycle drawing to a close, as her child-bear-
ing years come to an end. Since there is no relationship between the ability of the reproductive organs
to reproduce and the ability to enjoy sex, menopause
should not decrease a woman's interest in sex. The
sex drive does not die. The fact is, there is no reason
why a couple who has enjoyed marital relations reg-

ularly may not do so for years beyond the menopausal years.

Psychiatrists tell us that the sex act for a woman is usually successful because she *wants* it to be. Attitudes play the greatest part in healthy sex and marital relationships,[1] so a woman's attitude toward menopause will determine how it affects her marriage.

The Pluses

Many couples feel freer in their sexual relations after menopause. The fear of pregnancy is removed. For some couples, the end to the bother of menstruation each month is a relief. Usually the children are out of the house by these years, and there is more freedom in not having to structure romance into time slots revolving around others in the house.

The Minuses

With menopause, there are resultant physical changes because of the reduced estrogen levels. The ovaries and uterus shrink, muscles lose their elasticity, the vaginal walls get thinner, and reduction in lubrication may cause irritation during intercourse. Generous artificial lubricants and hormone creams can help to minimize irritation.

Hormone Replacement

Some unpleasant symptoms accompanying menopause may be alleviated by hormone replacement,

1. M. Edward Davis, *A Doctor Discusses Menopause and Estrogens* (Chicago: Budlong, 1983), p. 46.

but doctors are not agreed on its safety because of its side effects and possible link to cancer. The American Medical Association's Council on Scientific Affairs recently issued guidelines on estrogen use which recommend that it should be prescribed only when necessary, for the shortest possible time, and in the smallest possible dosage.[2]

A husband needs to help his wife through this period in her life by continuing to show an abundance of love, patience, and understanding. Because of her possible fears, his reassurance is needed to bolster and encourage her. She needs little expressions of kindnesses and appreciation to know she is still important to her husband.

Inhibitions

The place for modesty is *not* in marriage. A husband and wife need to learn to be completely open with one another and to get rid of any inhibitions that they may have brought to their marriage. These may include not undressing in front of each other, preferring sex in the dark because one would feel "dirty," having one's body seen by the other partner, or thinking sex should not be enjoyable because it is only for procreation.

Mutual Agreement

The truth of the matter is that within the bounds of marriage, anything is proper *as long as it is mu-*

2. Ibid., p. 58.

tually agreeable. God designed that a husband's and wife's bodies be appealing and pleasurable to each other, and experimenting and expanding on pleasurable possibilities can only enhance the sexual union.

Key to Full Enjoyment

There should be love and respect for one another's body, never demanding something of the other partner that he or she would not enjoy or would have guilt feelings about doing.

Weak Vagina Muscles

P.C. Muscle

As each wedding anniversary marks the passage of another year since a man and woman were joined in wedlock, so each year also stands as a reminder that sooner or later, a majority of married women have to face the problem of a weak, loose vagina, especially if they have had children. The cause will probably be due to the weakened pubococcygeus muscle (P.C. muscle). This muscle, along the pelvic floor, supports the pelvic organs which include the rectum, bladder, vagina, and uterus. The pelvic floor might be visualized as a muscular hammock slung from the pubic bone in front to the lower spine in back. Therefore, a weak, sagging, unsupportive P.C. muscle can result in problems of urinary control, loss of tone in the vaginal walls (which will decrease sexual pleasure during intercourse), and other problems.

The Solution

When this happens, a woman's first thought may be of going to her doctor for a tightening procedure. Tightening procedures tighten only the outer one-third of the vagina, mainly at the opening. They do not remedy the looseness of the inner two-thirds of the vagina, where the muscles need to be tight for the sexual enjoyment of both the husband and the wife.

The solution is to exercise the P.C. muscle using the Kegel exercises. These are named after Dr. Arnold Kegel, who was a surgeon and professor of gynecology in the 1940s. His purpose in prescribing this set of exercises was to correct a urinary leakage problem in a woman patient. An added happy result of the restrengthened muscles in his patient was a tightened vagina, giving more pleasure to the husband as well as the wife. In fact, reports came back from his patients that after using the exercises, many of them were experiencing orgasm for the first time in their lives!

These exercises can be done anytime, anywhere, and take only minutes a day. The procedure is to contract the P.C. muscle, hold it for a count of five or six, relax it, and then repeat the contraction, doing this for about two minutes and working up to a longer period of time.

Of course, the correct muscle must be exercised in order to receive the benefit of the Kegel exercises. One of the easiest ways to identify the P.C. muscle is to sit on the toilet with knees spread apart. Then, while urinating, stop the flow. Hold tightly for five seconds. Repeat this a number of times. If you can stop the flow completely, you are using the P.C. muscle. Once you are aware of the correct muscle, you can exercise anywhere. You can do it while riding in a car, while reading, washing dishes, or watching TV. Design your own plan. For instance, do ten in a row, three or four times a day. Gradually work up to two or three hundred a day. This may sound like a lot, but that would take only about ten minutes if you did them all at once. (And remember that you can be doing them while doing something else.) Do these for six to eight weeks. By then there should be remarkable improvement. Many women choose to continue some contractions each day after that time just to continue to keep the muscle tone good.

Many doctors recommend the Vagitone as an aid to a weak P.C. muscle. It can be purchased reasonably from Gyn-O-Tek, Inc., P.O. Box 29017, Portland, Oregon 97229-0017. This battery-powered device, electronically stimulates the pelvic muscles.

Note that a woman should not wait until after childbirth to undertake exercising the P.C. muscle as corrective therapy. Prevention is the best therapy. A young wife can keep her muscle tone good by establishing this habit right away in her marriage. Strong muscles will be able to support a baby during pregnancy and make delivery easier. This is why the Kegel exercises are a part of many natural childbirth classes, as well as the Lamaze hospital birth classes.

Strengthening the P.C. muscle may be the most important, kind, thoughtful, considerate, and loving thing you can do for your marriage. You cannot stop your biological clock from ticking, but by proper diet, nutrition, and exercise, you can extend your happy sex life well into your seventies—even longer! The importance of these factors is explained in the next chapter.

9

The Role of Nutrition, Weight, and Exercise in Sexuality

Sex and Obesity

We look at this subject for several reasons: (1) because of the effect overweight can have on a couple's sex life; and (2) because of the harm that carrying extra pounds can have on one's own physical health.

A recent report from the United States Select Committee on Nutrition and Human Needs concludes that the composition of the average American's diet has changed radically during this century. Fat and sugar consumption have risen to the point where these two dietary substances now make up at least 60 percent of the total caloric intake. At that level, fats and sugars are being used well in excess of the body's caloric requirements, thereby leading to the problem of obesity in the United States. The report further points out that obesity is a definite risk factor in cardiovascular disease, coronary disease, hypertension (high blood pressure), arteriosclerosis (hardening of the arteries), hernia, gallbladder disease, diabetes mellitus, and liver disease.[1]

Acknowledging the Problem

The problem often is getting oneself to admit that he or she is overweight. Overweight does not mean only thirty, forty, fifty, or more pounds over one's ideal weight. Two or three pounds should be dealt with just as quickly, lest those two or three pounds slowly lead to ten or twenty through the years. It is much easier to drop two or three pounds than to tackle those ten or twenty or more.

Effect on Sex Life

Obesity not only subjects the body to possible physical diseases, but can affect a couple's sex life.

We have seen that a man is aroused sexually primarily by his sight sense. Thus his visual appreciation of his wife must be appealing in order to enhance the sexual relationship. A woman who truly loves her husband will keep this fact in mind and work toward maintaining a sexually appealing appearance.

But the husband will not get off easily. He, too, is

1. Jay E. Satz, "Nutrition and Obesity," *Foods for Thought* (Nutri/System, July 1983).

urged to take care of his body. Though the wife is not as dependent as the husband on visual stimulation for arousal, a wife still appreciates a trim body that has been kept in shape.

Foolish Dieting

How does one lose unwanted pounds? A person could spend a lifetime trying every different diet offered in books and on the market and still not accomplish his or her goal. One of the authors spent a hilarious afternoon at a library looking at the books in the diet section. He counted at least 175 books that offered information on different kinds of diets, some of which the wildest imagination couldn't have dreamed up.

Crash diets are not good for a person's health, nor do they modify a person's behavioral habits in relation to eating. Although a person may lose a few pounds in that way, more often than not, those pounds quickly return.

Be a Calorie Cutter

The most effective way to lose weight is through a combination of calorie reduction and exercise, with a slow and gradual weight loss of only a few pounds per week. Find a chart that lists your height and ideal weight and the calories needed to maintain that weight. Then, by eating a balanced diet, reduce the calories you are eating in order to lose weight. For every thirty-six hundred calories cut, you should lose one pound. So reduce your calorie intake by only five hundred calories a day and lose one pound a week.

Reduce your intake by one thousand per day and lose two pounds a week.

Sex and Nutrition

Much study in recent years has brought out the correlation between sex and nutrition. Eating the proper foods is just as important as the amount of food consumed, since improper foods will deplete the body of nutrients needed to provide energy, not only for a healthy body but also for a healthy sex drive.

The Connection

What then is the connection between nutrition and sexual virility? Inside our bodies are glands that control our sex life. They are responsible for the normal functioning or malfunctioning of the sex organs. Glands need certain proteins, vitamins, minerals, and fatty acids in order to function properly. They must draw these substances from the foods we eat.[2] Therefore, there is a need to eat properly, in order to have optimum vitality, virility, fertility, and improved sexual vigor.

Eating properly means eating a well-balanced diet, consuming foods from all the basic food groups; trying to stay with as many fresh or frozen unprocessed foods as possible; avoiding the processed foods which have lost most of their nutritive value; cutting

2. Paavo O. Airola, *Sex and Nutrition* (New York: Charter Communications, 1970), p. 47.

down on the fats and sugars in one's diet; and eating less red meat and more fish and poultry.

Sex and Exercise

Exercise helps in a diet program, tones muscles, relieves tensions, improves appearance, and makes one generally feel better all over. More Americans than ever before can be found at the health spa, on the racquetball or handball courts, jogging, playing tennis, or in one of the many other avenues of physical fitness.

Telltale Signs

What of the relationship of exercise to sex? Exercise is essential to a good sex life. Out-of-shape, sagging muscles cannot be supportive nor cooperative during romantic sex. Muscles important for good sex are those in the abdominal area, the lower back, the pelvic region, and the gluteus muscles (buttocks). These should be strengthened, tightened, and maintained. A sagging stomach, a concave back, and spreading hips are telltale signs that some of these muscles are in poor shape and need attention.

Recommended Books

Several good books that deal specifically with exercise to strengthen the muscles used during intercourse are: *Sexercises Isometric and Isotonic*, and *Total Sexual Fitness for Women*. (*See* Bibliography.)

Lest men think they are exempt from this important maintenance of the body, the first book mentioned is devoted to exercises for both men and women. These books have pages and pages of photographs of specific, easy-to-follow exercises. Only five minutes a day will result in making romantic sex more pleasurable for you and your spouse.

Chapter 10 is devoted to frequently asked questions and the answers to those queries. Some of these have already been discussed in this book and the answers will refer the reader to the pertinent section. These are questions we most frequently hear in our clinic, private practices, and at lectures.

10

Frequently Asked Questions and Answers About Sex

1. *Do sexual temptations truly increase when couples are separated?*

   The Bible is very practical and warns couples not to be separated or to be apart. In fact in 1 Corinthians 7 it states that a couple should not be separated except for prayer and fasting, in order to avoid temptation.

2. *Is it important that both mates tell the other what pleases them sexually or should they both assume that the other knows?*

   It is *very* important that both husband and wife tell each other what pleases them in a sexual act. Since most people are very poor mind readers and since assumptions are often wrong, communication is vitally important.

3. *Is sexual pleasure in marriage okay, or is sex only for procreation?*

This seems to be a very naive question, but many Christian couples feel that sexual pleasure within marriage is wrong. Of course, within a marriage is where sex *should* be enjoyed. Unfortunately, our culture today has taken sex outside of the marriage, which has resulted in much grief, guilt, and actual complications in the sexual area. In Proverbs 5 (and other passages) God encourages married couples to enjoy sexual pleasures with each other "at all times."

4 *What is the average number of times per week for a young married couple to have intercourse?*

The average varies, naturally, depending on many factors—individual performance, ability of both individuals, and the subculture they come from. It has been said that about two to three times per week is the average for most couples. But again this may vary from several times per day to a few times per month depending on the couple.

5. *What are the phases of the female sexual response cycle?*

The first stage of the female sexual response cycle is the excitement phase, in which nipple erection and lubrication of the vaginal area will occur. The clitoris also increases in diameter during this time. The second is the plateau phase, where there is a sexual flush and also an increase in the size of the breasts. The third aspect is an orgasmic phase in which actual orgasm takes place. And finally, there is a resolution phase.

6. *What are the male response cycles?*

Basically, the male sexual response cycle is the same as in the female. There is an excitement phase, a plateau phase, an orgasmic phase, and a resolution phase. In the excitement phase there is an erection. In the plateau phase there is a sexual flush. And in the orgasmic phase there is the actual ejaculation orgasm. And then there is a resolution phase. The female is capable of multiple orgasms whereas the male is not because he has a longer refractory time.

7. *Is it true that hot showers may decrease the sperm count in the male?*

Yes. Hot showers may decrease the sperm count in the male, although naturally this may vary from one individual to another. If a couple is trying to conceive, the husband should not have a hot bath or hot shower just prior to intercourse.

8. *Is the hymen truly an indication of virginity in the female?*

It is true that the hymen is often broken during the first intercourse period. However, anatomy does vary, and it would be a mistake to take this as the only indication of virginity.

9. *Traditionally, what has been the major purpose of intercourse?*

Traditionally, one of the major purposes of sexual intercourse was, of course, reproduction. However, sexual intercourse should also be an expression of love and should be a means of enjoyment for the married couple, as seen in Proverbs 5.

10. *What is PMS or premenstrual syndrome, and does this affect the sexual response?*

Hormone changes do occur during the premenstrual period. The level of progesterone changes, and so does the level of norepinephrine which affects mood. Often the woman will be more irritable and/or depressed during this time. However, the degree of mood change may have a psychological factor. In summary, probably both physical and psychological factors are involved. Good psychotherapy will minimize the psychological causes of PMS symptoms.

11. *What can be done for PMS?*

Premenstrual syndrome may be treated by counseling. Sufferers also benefit by progesterone suppositories or other medications prescribed by a physician. Occasionally diuretics have been used. Some women may benefit from a special diet which eliminates sugars, caffeine and salt immediately before the menstrual period.

There is a thorough discussion on the medical aspects of PMS in *1250 Health-Care Ques-*

tions Women Ask by Joe S. McIlhaney, M.D. (See bibliography).

12. *What are the major positions that are used during sexual intercourse? (See chapter 4 for detailed answers to this question.)*

13. *Is it true that the clitoris is probably the most sensitive area and should be the major focus for orgasm?*

    While it is true that the clitoris is the most sensitive area in many women, it is probably a mistake to put too much emphasis on one part of the anatomy. Rather, let the woman enjoy what is natural for her regarding orgasms, whether it seems to be more of a vaginal or clitoral type of orgasm. One-third of wives experience orgasms only with the husband stimulating his wife's clitoris with his fingers gently for five to fifteen minutes.

14. *Are there any exercises that a female can do to increase enjoyment in the sexual act?*

    Yes. These have been traditionally called the Kegel exercises after Dr. Arnold H. Kegel, professor of gynecology at the USC School of Medicine. These are discussed in chapter 8, p. 118. Of course, it is also important to remember that much else can be done psychologically that also will improve the enjoyment of the sexual act, such as candlelight dinners, back rubs, and activities in the nude together.

15. *Are there any behavior techniques that can be done to help with premature ejaculation? (This is discussed in chapter 7, pp. 107-113.)*

16. *Are there any chemical substances that actually increase sex drive?*

No. These traditionally have been called "aphrodisiacs" and there are none that have a major effect on sex drive. Some people claim certain vitamins, foods, or chemicals increase the sex drive, but these are purely folklore and psychological in nature.

17. *Is infertility always caused by the female?*

A reliable estimate seems to indicate that perhaps 60 percent of the time infertility is caused by the female, and 40 percent of the time it is caused by the male. A lot of work has been done on infertility in recent years so that more and more help is available when a couple seeks help for infertility.

18. *What are the methods of birth control?*

One method that has a high success rate is, of course, the birth-control pill. It will approach 98 to 100 percent birth control. However, with any kind of medication or substances there are potential side effects and these side effects have to be weighed against the benefits.

The diaphragm (with or without foam) has also been used with a fairly high degree of success. Another method that has been used with a lot of success is the condom. This is perhaps the most available device and may have as high as an 80 percent success rate. The intrauterine devices formerly used widely throughout the world are now not recommended because they may cause infections and result in infertility. Also, it may be possible that they work by actually preventing an already fertilized egg from implanting in the uterus. Other methods used would include foam, douches, and the rhythm method. It should be stated that with the rhythm method there is a high percentage of pregnancies as well as lots of sexual frustration during the abstention periods.

19. *What are the side effects of the birth-control pill?*

Birth control pills have several possible side effects. For example, blood clots are possible. It is also possible for an individual to become depressed on birth-control pills. However, overall, the pill has proven to be quite safe for most users.

20. *Are vasectomies effective in providing birth control?*

Usually. However, it is important to realize that sperm will still be passed for several ejaculations after a vasectomy. It is also important to realize that a vasectomy will affect some men psychologically, and counseling should be sought before a vasectomy is done. The same is true regarding women who have their fallopian tubes tied so that pregnancy cannot take place. This procedure may have a psychological effect on some females and counseling should be done prior to this.

21. *What is the most commonly and widely used method of birth control in the world?*

The condom. There are several reasons for this: it is convenient, safe, economical, and has no side effects. And it is most effective in preventing sexually transmitted diseases, especially when used in combination with foam. Of course, the disadvantages are described as decreased sensation for the husband and interrupted foreplay.

22. *What does the Bible mean when it refers to a man and woman becoming "one flesh"?*

When a man and woman marry and have intercourse they actually become one flesh, in a sense, in God's eyes. Thus, it is very important that marriage be held in high regard. It is also very important that the couple keep themselves, sexually, just for each other, because when affairs take place a person becomes a part of the individual with whom he or she has the affair and in a sense, actually gives himself or herself to that individual.

23. *What are the parts of the female genitalia?*

Briefly, the parts of the female genitalia are: the external genitalia, the labia minora and labia majora (the external lips of the skin); and the internal genitalia, which are made up of the two ovaries, the ovary ducts, the uterus, and the vagina. The ovaries contain thousands of female eggs. The ovaducts have been described as the fallopian tubes. Each is about four inches long and is essential to transport the female egg. The uterus is a muscular womb.

The two ovaducts open near the top of the uterus.

The tube of the uterus is the cervix which should be checked with an annual pap smear for cancer.

The vagina is an elastic canal about four or five inches long, containing little glands. These glands provide lubrication during sexual intercourse.

The hymen is a membrane which may be broken during the time of initial intercourse, which may cause some pain. The husband should be sensitive to this on the honeymoon.

The urethra is an outlet for the urine from the bladder. It may become infected because of bruising during intercourse.

The clitoris is enclosed in a shaft and is a very sensitive area also during intercourse. It is enlarged when it is caressed by the male.

The pubococcygeus (PC) muscles are muscles that have a lot to do with the enjoyment of the sex act. Exercises to strengthen these muscles were described earlier.

24. *How would you describe the male sex organs?*

The male sex organs consist of the penis, scrotum, and the ducts. The penis consists of erectile tissue which is distended with blood during intercourse. During circumcision (usually done on the eighth day after birth, because the blood clotting factors are 150 percent of normal on that day), the skin over the head of the penis is cut back. The testes are about one-and-one-half by one-half inch in size inside the scrotum. They produce sperm and thus are important in reproduction.

25. *What are some common-sense factors that are important in the sex act?*

It is important to realize that sex has much to do with the state of mind. Love, romance, and kindness are very important. It is also important to remember such things as soap, perfume, toothpaste, and shaving cream.

26. *What is incest?*

Incest refers to intercourse between members of the same family. The Bible condemns this. It causes great psychological problems among its participants and other family members. And, if pregnancy occurs, the weak genes shared by close relatives are likely to produce an ill-formed or retarded baby.

27. *What is exhibitionism?*

An exhibitionist derives sexual enjoyment from exposing himself.

28. *What is voyeurism?*

Voyeurists' key to sexual excitement is watching sexual acts committed. While pornography has become a big business, it is a cause of sexual problems.

29. *What is pedophilia?*

Pedophilia is a sex act with a child.

30. *What is bestiality?*

Bestiality is intercourse with an animal.

31. *Is it true that women who have premarital affairs are more likely to have extramarital affairs?*

Yes. One sexual sin usually leads to another.

32. Is homosexual activity wrong?

The Bible takes a very strong stand against homosexuality. Such passages as Romans 1 (and others) indicate that it is very wrong. God intended that a male marry a female and then the two should engage in the sexual act. In addition, it should be mentioned that even in religious society there has been a decrease in emphasis on affairs as being wrong. Affairs between a man and woman outside of marriage not only are wrong but they also usually will decrease the sexual enjoyment in the marriage.

33. What is fetishism?

Fetishism is achieving sexual excitement from an inanimate object.

34. What is a transvestite?

Transvestites achieve sexual gratification from wearing clothes of the opposite sex.

35. What are masochism and sadism?

The masochist obtains his enjoyment from being hurt. And a sadist arrives at sexual enjoyment by hurting others.

36. What percent of females reach orgasm?

Perhaps 70 percent of all females reach orgasm. Nearly 100 percent of females can achieve orgasms with proper psychotherapy.

37. What is impotence?

Impotence is the inability on the male's part to have an orgasm because of trouble obtaining an erection. This may be caused by physical or psychological factors. Proper therapy can usually correct this problem. (*See* chapter 6.)

38. *Is it true that most men beyond the age of fifty or sixty are impotent?*

No. If impotence is involved at any age it should be checked out for correctible physical or psychological factors.

39. *Is it true that after menopause there is an end to orgasms?*

No. Women do experience orgasms after menopause.

40. *Is it true that men who have a prostatectomy cannot experience orgasms?*

Most men who have prostatectomies do very well having orgasms afterwards. A few may have difficulty. It is advisable to discuss possible problems with the surgeon beforehand.

41. *Should intercourse during pregnancy be avoided to avert possible danger to the fetus?*

In general, there is very little danger to having intercourse during pregnancy. Of course, during the last few weeks, you should consult your doctor for specific advice.

42. *Is it true that prostitutes have an increased sex drive?*

No. Prostitutes usually have no sex drive whatsoever. Probably the couples who enjoy sex the most are those who follow the principles of keeping sex within the marriage. Sex is beautiful within the marriage but problems can develop outside the marriage. The Bible gives very practical solutions here.

43. *Is romance an important factor in selection of a mate?*

    Certainly romance is an important factor in choosing a mate. However, what many couples fail to recognize is that other factors are also very significant. It is often important that couples come from similar backgrounds, and it is certainly very critical that they have similar goals in life.

44. *Can an individual who has had a heart attack (a myocardial infarction) engage in intercourse?*

    The vast majority of men and women after MIs can later begin to have intercourse again. Of course, your physician should be consulted.

45. *Are all men interested only in sex?*

    Extreme statements are usually wrong. All men are not interested in sex alone, just like all women are not evil. Personalities vary from individual to individual. The sex act, of course, is important to both the male and the female within the marriage situation. It is true that men may be somewhat more oriented to the physical side of marriage while women may be somewhat more oriented toward love and security. However, both are important to each other.

46. *Do women who experience sexual enjoyment in marriage before menopause continue to have sexual enjoyment after menopause?*

    Yes, they do. It is a misunderstanding to think that sexual interest and activity decrease after menopause.

47. *Is the wife's view of herself as being attractive important in the sex act?*

Self-image and viewing herself as being attractive is important for the wife. Thus, it is important for the husband to remember this and to build up his wife and give her good feedback. In other words, for the wife to act sexy in the sex act, she needs to feel that way.

48. *What is intimacy?*

Intimacy is very important within the marriage. It involves several factors. First of all, it involves a commitment to each other. It involves a commitment to stay in the marriage regardless of what happens. Intimacy also involves self-disclosure and a willingness to talk about oneself. It involves a display of affection and love, as well as the freedom to share temporary angry feelings tactfully ("speaking the truth in love"). Intimacy involves a couple feeling like a team going through life together. Intimacy involves many factors which are of utmost importance in the sexual act.

49. *Is it true that sexual promiscuity has increased in recent years?*

Certainly. In the 1970s, for example, the vast majority of Americans felt that extramarital sex was okay. In the early 1950s perhaps only 30 percent of females had premarital intercourse. Over two-thirds had premarital intercourse in the 1970s. However, with the increased recent concern to avoid AIDS and other sexually transmitted diseases, there seems to be a corresponding decrease in pre-marital sex.

50. *How effective is withdrawal as a method of contraception?*

What many young couples do not realize is that sperm may be emitted from the penis prior to the actual ejaculation itself. Thus withdrawal as a method of birth control is not effective.

51. *Does it help to give estrogen to post-menopausal women?*

Yes. Because estrogen helps to prevent bone demineralization, and it also may help lubrication in the vagina. Estrogen will not usually elevate mood swings or have a major effect on the sex drive itself.

52. *What are the most common organic causes of impotence?*

Probably the most common are: scleroderma (hardening of the skin), diabetes mellitus, and prostate surgery.

53. *Are there any tests to determine whether impotence is organic or psychogenic in origin?*

Yes, some tests do help to differentiate the two. However, even with the test there is often confusion. The nocturnal penile tumescence monitor is one test that is used to determine if an individual has the ability to have an erection during the night.

54. *Does vascular disease ever cause impotence?*

Yes, vascular disease can be one cause of

impotence. It is something that your doctor should explore.

55. *What are some things that a workup for impotence would include?*

Workup for impotence would probably include an in-depth history as well as a test for blood-sugar level. It might include arteriography (making a film record of the arteries), the nocturnal penile tumescence monitor, cystometric (bladder) evaluations, and a plasma- or urinary-hormonal essay.

56. *Is it true that perhaps as many as 25 percent of all couples experiencing infertility are able to conceive after having an initial workup?*

Yes. Many couples can then conceive.

57. *Is foreplay important in the sex act?*

Foreplay is usually very important in the sex act. In general, men often are not sensitive enough in this area. Most husbands should spend more time in foreplay.

58. *Do orgasms have to be simultaneous?*

No. Orgasms do not have to come at the same time. In fact, trying to do this may actually prevent orgasms and cause sexual problems.

59. *Is promiscuity in the female teenager an indication of a strong sex drive?*

No. Usually promiscuity in the female teenager indicates a strong need to be reassured that she is really cared for. Lack of attention and appropriate affection from an absent or busy father is a common cause. In other words, she substitutes a physical relationship for the emotional relationship that she truly craves. She truly wants to know that someone really cares for her. Often she ends up feeling that men love her only for her body, rather than truly loving *her*. She may even be attracted to self-centered males who reinforce her prejudice.

60. *When should sex education take place in the home in raising children?*

Probably either extreme is to be avoided. When a young child has questions in the sexual area, they should be answered in a factual and caring manner right then. To go to the extreme of always avoiding discussion of sexual issues probably will cause damage. Also, to push a lot of information on young children before they ask for it will result in confusion, and even cause damage.

61. *Why do partners in a marriage have extramarital affairs?*

All individuals feel insecure to some degree, and all individuals feel inferior to some degree. One way to attempt to overcome these inferiority feelings is through sexual conquests (what the Bible refers to as the "lust of the flesh"). If an individual feels inferior, he or she may temporarily feel better by having an affair with someone who seems sexually attractive. Of course, in the long run, this leaves the person feeling more inferior and having more problems with low self-worth and true guilt. God's ways are always best in the long run.

62. *On which day during the female cycle is pregnancy most likely to occur?*

Pregnancy is most likely to occur on the fourteenth day after the period begins. However, since there is tremendous variation from individual to individual as to exactly when the egg travels down the fallopian tube, it seems that pregnancy can occur at almost any time. Also, the male's sperm sometimes stays alive in the uterus for several days after intercourse. Therefore, the rhythm method of birth control is a poor one.

63. *Is there any way the Christian husband can enhance his orgasms when he is having sex?*

One of the best aids for the husband is for his wife to fondle the penis five to ten minutes before actual intercourse. This will usually double the pleasure of orgasm for the husband.

64. *Should a Christian married couple ever have sex during the wife's menstrual period?*

This is something each couple will need to decide for themselves. There are no clear New Testament commandments on this. However, it was discouraged in the Old Testament laws, probably because of what blood symbolized.

65. *With the increase and the emphasis on sex today on TV, is romance in sex a major quality that an individual looks for in a mate?*

No. Research shows that the major quality individuals are seeking in their partners is *love*.

Perhaps they often view sex as a way to obtain the love they want. In the Bible God gives an excellent plan regarding the whole issue of sex and love. God's desire is that a couple be committed only to each other in the sexual union within the marriage. With a commitment to each other and with the love they have for each other, naturally sexual enjoyment also increases.

66. *What is frigidity?*

Frigidity is the inability to perform in sex. Some therapists estimate that it occurs in as high as 50 percent of first marriages. Doctor and Mrs. Ed Wheat in their excellent book, *Intended for Pleasure*, describe several ways to overcome this problem. They encourage (1) having a private place for sexual intercourse and being sure that both parties are clean, (2) having a place that is restful and free of stress, (3) taking off all of one's clothes, the husband first and then the wife.

We would add that talking about any deep-seated fears and resolving them will help in getting rid of frigidity. It is important to the wife who is experiencing frigidity, initially, to simply spend time, take walks, and hold hands with her husband. In other words, move gradually from the most nonthreatening situation to the most threatening, which is intercourse.

67. *In a female with frigidity, what is more important, an orgasm or the enjoyment of the sex act?*

The most important thing with frigidity in

the female is learning to enjoy the sex act. If she does this, then the orgasms will usually occur naturally. However, if she focuses on having an orgasm, this may actually prevent having the orgasm itself.

68. *When an individual in a marriage has a sexual problem, is it only his or her problem, or is it a problem of the couple?*

When one mate has a problem in the sexual area of the marriage both mates have a problem, and it is a common problem. There should be a commitment to work on solving it together. If it cannot be resolved by reading a book, such as this one, the couple should carefully select a biblically oriented Christian psychiatrist, psychologist, or sex therapist.

11

Conclusion

In these chapters we have shared with you the findings of the authors: Richard Meier, a former pastor (with twenty-eight years of pastoral experience) and now a marriage counselor; his wife, Lorraine, who began counseling during her many years as a pastor's wife; Frank Minirth, M.D., president of the Minirth-Meier Clinic in Richardson, Texas, and a former professor of pastoral counseling; and Paul Meier, M.D., vice president of the clinic, also a former seminary professor.

Although we have repeatedly reminded you throughout this book that sexual happiness in marriage is a part of God's plan for us, we must remind husbands and wives to keep the lines of communication open, not only to each other, but to God, his Holy Spirit, and his Son. Praying together is one way of keeping in touch with the Great Communicator.

Your pastor, professional counselor, and (we hope) this book, will help you understand and solve any problems of a sexual nature which may arise in your marriage. However, it is by asking for the help of the Holy Spirit and giving him entrance to your hearts that your marriage will become more beautiful.

Make no mistake about it, sex and marriage go together. As the song says, "You can't have one without the other."

"As marriage represents a sacred covenant, so sex is the seal of that covenant ... This is God's appointed bond for the most intimate and sacred of human relationships.[1])

> ... And God saw that it was good.
> Genesis 1:12

1. Dwight Hervey Small, *Christian: Celebrate Your Sexuality* (Old Tappan, N.J.: Fleming H Revell, 1974), p. 205.

Bibliography

In doing our research we found some books that, while we wouldn't classify them as "Christian," are useful. The Lord reminds us that in some areas of life, "The children of this world are in their generation wiser than the children of light" (Luke 16:8). We are glad, however, that subjects included in these books are being discussed more openly by qualified Christian specialists. This bibliography, then, includes both secular and Christian books.

Airola, Paavo O. *Sex and Nutrition.* New York: Charter Communications, 1970.

Blumstein, Philip, and Pepper Schwartz. "Couples: The American Way of Loving." *Redbook* 161 (September 1983):75–77.

Butler, Robert N., and Myrna Lewis. *Sex After Sixty.* Boston: G.K. Hall & Co., 1977.

Castleman, Michael. *Sexual Solutions*. New York: Simon and Schuster, 1983.

Crenshaw, Theresa Larsen. *Bedside Manners*. New York: McGraw-Hill, 1983.

Davis, M. Edward, and Dona Meilach. *A Doctor Discusses Menopause and Estrogens*. Chicago: Budlong, 1983.

Diagram Group. *Sex: A User's Manual*. New York: G.P. Putnam's Sons, 1981.

Dunbar, Robert E. *A Doctor Discusses a Man's Sexual Health*. Chicago: Budlong, 1976.

Goodman, Eric K. "The Sexual Fears That Haunt Men." *Woman's Day* (5 July 1983).

Jacobs, Leo I. *Overcoming Impotence*. Chicago: Contemporary Books, 1978.

LaHaye, Tim and Beverly. *The Act of Marriage: The Beauty of Married Love*. Grand Rapids: Zondervan, 1976.

Lance, Kathryn, and Maria Agardy. *Total Sexual Fitness for Women*. New York: Rawson Wade Publishers, 1981.

Mayhall, Jack and Carol. *Marriage Takes More Than Love*. Colorado Springs: Navpress, 1978.

McIlhaney, Joe S. *1250 Health-Care Questions Women Ask*. Grand Rapids: Baker, 1985.

Miles, Herbert J. and Ruth Harrington Miles. *Husband-Wife Equality*. Old Tappan, N.J.: Fleming H. Revell Co., 1978.

Morgenstern, Michael. *How to Make Love to a Woman*. New York: Ballantine Books, 1982.

O'Relly, Edward. *Sexercises Isometric and Isotonic*. New York: Bell Publishing, 1967.

Penner, Clifford and Joyce. *The Gift of Sex*. Waco, Tex.: Word, 1981.

Reuben, David. *How to Get More Out of Sex*. New York: David McKay Co., 1974.

Roen, Philip. *Male Sexual Health.* New York: Morrow, 1974.

Satz, Jay E. "Nutrition and Obesity." *Foods for Thought.* Nutri/System, July 1983.

Ser Vass, Cory. "Prostate Cancer, A National Tragedy." *The Saturday Evening Post* 255 (October 1983):26.

Small, Dwight Hervey. *Christian: Celebrate Your Sexuality.* Old Tappan, N.J.: Fleming H. Revell Co., 1974.

Wheat, Ed and Gaye. *Intended for Pleasure.* Old Tappan, N.J.: Fleming H. Revell Co., 1981.

Willy, A., L. Vander, and O. Fisher. *The Illustrated Encyclopedia of Sex.* New York: Cadillac Publishing, 1950.

Richard Meier, D.Min., a former pastor, is a marriage counselor and popular seminar speaker. **Lorraine Meier,** Richard's wife, began counseling women during her many years as a pastor's wife. **Frank Minirth, M.D.,** is president and founder of the Minirth Clinic in Richardson, Texas. **Paul Meier,** M.D., is vice president of the Minirth Meier New Life Clinic in Richardson, Texas.